The Spiritual Combat

The Classic Manual on Spiritual Warfare

by
Dom Lorenzo Scupoli

First published in 1589 A.D

The Spiritual Combat
by Father Dom Lorenzo Scupoli
Copyright © 2020 Holy Water Books

ISBN-13: 978-1-950782-10-9
All rights reserved.
Holy Water Books (Publisher)

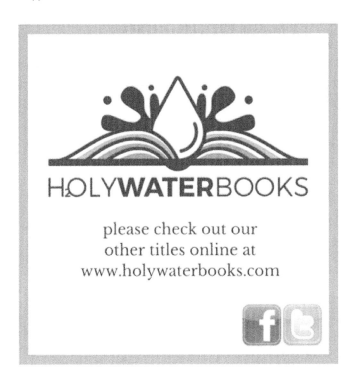

HOLYWATERBOOKS

please check out our
other titles online at
www.holywaterbooks.com

None is vanquished in this spiritual combat,
but he who ceases to struggle and loses confidence in God.
"He does not receive the Victor's Crown unless he fights well"
(2 Timothy 2:5)

The Spiritual Combat
Table of Contents

Introduction

I: Of the Essence of Christian Perfection - Of the Struggle Requisite for its Attainment - And of the Four Things Needful in this Conflict

Would you attain in Christ the height of perfection, and by a nearer and nearer approach to God become one spirit with Him? Before undertaking this greatest and noblest of all imaginable enterprises, you must first learn what constitutes the true and perfect spiritual life. For many have made it to consist exclusively in austerities, maceration of the flesh, hair-shirts, disciplines, long vigils and fasts, and other like bodily hardships and penance's. Others, especially women, fancy they have made great progress therein, if they say many vocal prayers, hear many Masses and long Offices, frequent many churches, receive many communions. Others (and those sometimes among cloistered religious) are persuaded that perfection depends wholly upon punctual attendance in choir, upon silence, solitude, and regularity. And thus, some in these, others in various similar actions, suppose that the foundations of perfection may be laid.

But it is not so indeed; for as some of these are means to acquire grace, others fruits of grace, they cannot be held to constitute Christian perfection and the true life of grace. They are unquestionably most powerful means, in the hands of those who use them well and discreetly, of acquiring grace in order to gain strength and vigor against their own sinfulness and weakness, to defend themselves against our common enemies, to supply all those spiritual aids so necessary to all the servants of God, and especially to beginners in the spiritual life. Again, they are fruits of grace in truly spiritual persons, who chastise the body because it has o ended its Creator, and in order to keep it low and submissive in His service; who keep silence and live solitary that they may avoid the slightest offense against their Lord, and converse with heaven; who attend divine worship, and give themselves to works of piety; who pray and meditate on the life and passion of our Lord, not from curiosity or sensible pleasure, but that they may know better and more deeply their own sinfulness, and the goodness and mercy of God, enkindle ever more and more within their hearts the love of God and the hatred of themselves, following the Son of God with the Cross upon their shoulders in the way of self-abnegation; who frequent the holy sacraments, to the glory of His Divine Majesty, to unite them- selves more closely with God, and to gain new strength against His enemies.

But these external works, though all most holy in themselves, may yet, by the fault of those who use them as the foundation of their spiritual building, prove a more fatal occasion of ruin than open sins. Such persons leave their hearts unguarded to the mercy of their own inclinations, and exposed to the lurking deceits of the devil, who, seeing them out of the direct road, not only lets them continue these exercises with satisfaction, but leads them in their own vain imagination to expatiate on the delights of paradise, and to fancy themselves to be borne aloft amidst the angelic choir and to feel God within them. Sometimes they find themselves absorbed in high, or mysterious, and ecstatic meditations, and, forgetful of the world and of all that it contains, they believe themselves to be caught up to the third heaven.

But the life and conversation of such Persons prove the depth of the delusion in which they are held, and their great distance from the perfection after which we are inquiring; for in all things, great and small, they desire to be preferred and placed above others; they are wedded to their own opinion, and obstinate in their own will; and blind to their own faults, they are busy and diligent observers and critics of the deeds and words of others.

But touch only with a finger their point of honor, a certain vain estimation in which they hold themselves and would have others to hold them, interrupt their stereotyped devotions, and they are disturbed and o ended beyond measure.

And if, to bring them back to the true knowledge of themselves and of the way of perfection, Almighty God should send them sickness, or sorrow, or persecution (that touchstone of His servants' loyalty, which never befalls them without His permission or command), then is the unstable foundation of their spiritual edifice discovered, and its interior, all corroded and defaced by pride, laid bare; for they refuse to resign themselves to the will of God, to acquiesce in His always righteous though mysterious judgments, in all events, whether joyful or sorrowful, which may befall them; neither will they, after the example of His Divine Son in His sufferings and humiliation, abase themselves below all creatures, accounting their persecutors as beloved friends, as instruments of God's goodness, and cooperators with Him in the mortification. perfection, and salvation of their souls.

Hence it is most certain that such persons are in serious danger; for, the inward eye being darkened, wherewith they con- template themselves and these their external good works, they attribute to themselves a very high degree of perfection; and thus puffed up with pride they pass judgment upon others, while a very extraordinary degree of God's assisting grace is needed to convert themselves. For the open sinner is more easily converted and restored to God than the man who shrouds himself under the cloak of seeming virtue.

You see, then, very clearly that, as I have said, the spiritual life consists not in these things. It consists in nothing else but the knowledge of the goodness and the greatness of God, and of our nothingness and inclination to all evil; in the love of Him and the hatred of ourselves, in subjection, not to Him alone, but for love of Him, to all His creatures; in entire renunciation of all will of our own and absolute resignation to all His divine pleasure; and furthermore, willing and doing all this purely for the glory of God and solely to please Him, and because He so wills and merits thus to be loved and served.

This is the law of love, impressed by the hand of the Lord Himself upon the hearts of His faithful servants; this is the abnegation of self which He requires of us; this is His sweet yoke and light burden; this is the obedience to which, by His voice and His example, our Master and Redeemer calls us. In aspiring to such sublime perfection you will have to do continual violence to yourself by a generous conflict with your own will in all things, great or small, until it be wholly annihilated; you must prepare yourself, therefore, for the battle with all readiness of mind; for none but brave warriors shall receive the crown.

This is indeed the hardest of all struggles; for while we strive against self, self is striving against us, and therefore is the victory here most glorious and precious in the sight of God. For if you will set yourself to trample down and exterminate all your unruly appetites, desires, and wishes, even in the smallest and most inconsiderable matters, you will render a greater and more acceptable service to God than if you should discipline yourself to blood, fast more rigorously than hermits or anchorites of old, or convert millions of souls, and yet voluntarily leave even one of these evils alive within you. For although the conversion of souls is no doubt more precious to the Lord than the mortification of a fancy, nevertheless nothing should in your sight be of greater account than to will and to do that very thing which the Lord specially demands and requires of you. And He will infallibly be better pleased that you should watch and labor to mortify your passions than if, consciously and willfully leaving but one alive within you, you should serve Him in some other matter of greater importance in itself.

Now that you see wherein Christian perfection consists, and that it requires a continual sharp warfare against self, you must provide yourself with four most sure and necessary weapons, in order to secure the palm and gain the victory in this spiritual combat.

These weapons are:
- ❖ Distrust of self (diffidence of ourselves);
- ❖ Trust in God (confidence in God);
- ❖ Exercise; and
- ❖ Prayer.

Of all these we will, with the Divine assistance, treat briefly and plainly.

The First Two Weapons of the Spiritual Combat

II: Distrust of Self (diffidence)

So necessary is self-distrust in this conflict, that without it you will be unable, I say not to achieve the victory desired, but even to overcome the very least of your passions. And let this be well impressed upon your mind; for our corrupt nature too easily inclines us to a false estimate of ourselves; so that, being really nothing, we account ourselves to be something, and presume, without the slightest foundation, upon our own strength.

This is a fault not easily discerned by us, but very displeasing in the sight of God. For He desires and loves to see in us a frank and true recognition of this most certain truth, that all the virtue and grace which is within us is derived from Him alone, Who is the fountain of all good, and that nothing good can proceed from us, no, not even a thought which can find acceptance in His sight.

And although this very important self-distrust is itself the work of His Divine Hand, and is bestowed upon His beloved, now by means of holy inspirations, now by sharp chastisements and violent and almost irresistible temptations, and by other means which we ourselves do not understand; still it is His will that we on our part should do all in our power to attain it. I therefore set before you four methods, by the use of which, in dependence always on Divine grace, you may acquire this gift.

❖ The first is, to know and consider your own vileness and nothingness, and your inability of yourself to do any good, by which to merit an entrance into the kingdom of heaven.

❖ The second, continually to ask it of the Lord in fervent and humble prayer; for it is His gift. And in order to reach its attainment we must look upon ourselves not only as destitute thereof, but as of ourselves incapable of acquiring it. Present yourself, therefore, continually before the Divine Majesty, with an assured faith that He is willing of His great goodness to grant your petition; wait patiently all the time which His Providence appoints, and without doubt you shalt obtain it.

❖ The third is, to stand in fear of your own judgment about yourself, of your strong inclination to sin, of the countless hosts of enemies against whom you are incapable of making the slight- est resistance, of their long practice in open warfare and secret stratagem, of their transformations into angels of light, and of the innumerable arts and stares which they secretly spread for us even in the very way of holiness.

❖ The fourth is, whenever you art overtaken by any fault, to look more deeply into yourself, and more keenly feel your absolute and utter weakness; for to this end did God permit your fall, that, warned by His inspiration and illumined by a clearer light than before, you may come to know yourself, and learn to despise yourself as a thing unutterably vile, and be therefore also willing to be so accounted and despised by others. For without this willingness there can be no holy self-distrust, which is founded on true humility and experimental self-knowledge.

This self-knowledge is clearly needful to all who desire to be united to the Supreme Light and Uncreated Truth; and the

Divine Clemency often makes use of the fall of proud and presumptuous men to lead to It; justly suffering them to fall into some faults which they trusted to avoid by their own strength, that they may learn to know and absolutely distrust themselves. Our Lord is not, however, wont to use so severe a method, until those more gracious means of which we have before spoken have failed to work the cure designed by His Divine Mercy. He permits a man to fall more or less deeply in proportion to his pride and self-esteem; so that if there were no presumption (as in the case of the Blessed Virgin Mary), there would be no fall. Therefore, whenever you shall fall, take refuge at once in humble self-knowledge, and beseech the Lord with urgent entreaties to give you light truly to know yourself, and entire self-distrust, lest you should fall again perhaps into deeper perdition.

III: Of Trust in God (confidence)

Self-distrust, necessary as we have shown it to be in this conflict, is not alone sufficient. Unless we would be put to flight, or remain helpless and vanquished in the hands of our enemies, we must add to it perfect trust in God, and expect from Him alone succor and victory. For as we, who are nothing, can look for nothing from ourselves but falls, and therefore should utterly distrust ourselves; so from our Lord may we assuredly expect complete victory in every conflict. To obtain His help, let us therefore arm ourselves with a lively confidence in Him.

And this also may be accomplished in four ways:

❖ First, by asking it of God.

❖ Secondly, by gazing with the eye of faith at the infinite wisdom and omnipotence of God, to which nothing is impossible or di cult, and con ding in His unbounded goodness and unspeakable willingness to give, hour-by-hour and moment-by-moment, all things needful for the spiritual life, and perfect victory over ourselves, if we will but throw ourselves with confidence into His Arms. For how shall our Divine Shepherd, Who followed after His lost sheep for three-and-thirty years with loud and bitter cries through that painful and thorny way, wherein He spilt His Heart's Blood and laid down His life how shall He refuse to turn His quickening glance upon the poor sheep which now follows Him in obedience to His commands, or with a desire (though sometimes faint and feeble) to obey Him! When it cries to Him piteously for help, will He not hear, and laying it upon His Divine Shoulders, call upon His friends and all the angels of heaven to rejoice with Him? For if our Lord ceased not to search most diligently for the blind and deaf sinner, the lost drachma of the gospel, till He found him; can He abandon him who, like a lost sheep, cries and calls piteously upon his Shepherd? And if God knocks continually at the heart of man, desiring to enter in and sup there, and to communicate to it His gifts, who can believe that when that heart opens and invites Him to enter, He will turn a deaf ear to the invitation, and refuse to come in?

❖ Thirdly, the third way to acquire this holy confidence is, to call to mind that truth so plainly taught in Holy Scripture, that no one who trusted in God has ever been confounded.

❖ The fourth, which will serve at once towards the attainment of self-distrust and of trust in God, is this: when any duty presents itself to be done, any struggle with self to be made, any victory over self to be attempted, before proposing or resolving upon it, think first upon your own weakness; next turn, full of self-distrust, to the wisdom, the power, and the goodness of God; and in reliance upon these, resolve to labor and to fight generously. Then, with these weapons in your hands, and with the help of prayer (of which we shall speak in its proper place), set yourself to labor and to strive.

Unless you observe this order, though you may seem to yourself to be doing all things in reliance upon God, you will too often find yourself mistaken; for so common is a presumptuous self-confidence, and so subtle are the forms it assumes, that it lurks almost always even under an imagined self-distrust and fancied confidence in God.

To avoid presumption as much as possible, and in order that all your works may be wrought in distrust of self and trust in God, the consideration of your own weakness must precede the consideration of God's omnipotence; and both together must precede all your actions.

IV: How a man may know whether he is active in Self-Distrust and Trust in God

The presumptuous servant often supposes that he has acquired self-distrust and trust in God when the case is far otherwise.

And this will be made clear to thee by the effect produced on thy mind by a fall. If thou art so saddened and disquieted thereby as to be tempted to despair of making progress or doing good, it is a sure sign that thy trust is in self and not in God. For he who has any large measure of self-distrust and trust in God feels neither surprise, nor despondency, nor bitterness, when he falls; for he knows that this has arisen from his own weakness and want of trust in God. On the contrary, being, rendered thereby more distrustful of self, more humbly con dent in God, detesting above all things his fault and the unruly passions which have occasioned it, and mourning with a quiet, deep, and patient sorrow over his offense against God, he pursues his enterprise, and follows after his enemies, even to the death, with a spirit more resolute and undaunted than before.

I would that these things were well considered by certain

persons so called spiritual, who cannot and will not be at rest when they have fallen into any fault. They rush to their spiritual father, rather to get rid of the anxiety and uneasiness which spring from wounded self-love than for that purpose which should be their chief end in seeking him, to purify themselves from the stain of sin, and to fortify themselves against its power by means of the most Holy Sacrament of Penance.

V: Of the Error of Many, Who Mistake Faint-heartedness for a Virtue

Many also deceive themselves in this way, they mistake the fear and uneasiness which follow after sin for virtuous emotions; and know not that these painful feelings spring from wounded pride, and a presumption which rests upon confidence in themselves and their own strength. They have accounted themselves to be something, and relied unduly upon their own powers. Their fall proves to them the vanity of this self-dependence, and they are immediately troubled and astonished as at some strange thing, and are disheartened at seeing the prop to which they trusted suddenly give way.

This can never befall the humble man, who trusts in his God alone, and in nothing presumes upon himself. Though grieved when he falls into a fault, he is neither surprised nor disquieted; for he knows that his own misery and weakness, already clearly manifest to himself by the light of truth, have brought all this upon him.

VI: Further directions how to attain Self-Distrust and Trust in God

Since our whole power to subdue our enemies arises principally from self-distrust and trust in God, I will give you some further directions to enable you, by the Divine Assistance, to acquire it. Know, then, for a certain truth, that neither all gifts, natural or acquired, nor all graces given gratis, nor the knowledge of all Scripture, nor long habitual exercise in the service of God, will enable us to do His will, unless in every good and acceptable work to be performed, in every temptation to be overcome, in every peril to be avoided, in every Cross to be borne in conformity to His will, our heart be sustained and up-borne by an especial aid from Him, and His hand be outstretched to help us. We must, then, bear this in mind all our life long, every day, every hour, every moment, that we may never indulge so much as a thought of self-confidence.

And as to confidence in God, know that it is as easy to Him to conquer many enemies as few; the old and experienced as the weak and young.

Therefore we will suppose a soul to be heavy-laden with sins, to have every possible fault and every imaginable defect, and to have tried, by every possible means and every kind of Spiritual Exercise, to forsake sin and to practice holiness. We will suppose this soul to have done all this, and yet to have failed in making the smallest advance in holiness, nay, on the contrary, to have been borne the more strongly towards evil.

For all this she must not lose her trust in God, nor give over her spiritual conflict and lay down her arms, but still fight on resolutely, knowing that none is vanquished in this spiritual com- bat but he who ceases to struggle and loses confidence in God, whose succor never fails His soldiers, though He sometimes permits them to be wounded. Fight on, then, valiantly; for on this depends the whole issue of the strife; for there is a ready and effectual remedy for the wounds of all combatants who look confidently to God and to His aid for help; and when they least expect it they shall see their enemies dead at their feet.

The Third Weapon of the Spiritual Combat

VII: Of Spiritual Exercises and first of the Exercise of the Understanding, which must be kept guarded against ignorance and curiosity

I f in this warfare we are provided with no weapons except self-distrust and trust in God, needful as both these are, we shall not only fail to gain the victory over ourselves, but shall fall into many evils. To these, therefore, we must add the use of Spiritual Exercises, the third weapon named above.

And these relate chiefly to the Understanding and the Will. As regards the Understanding, we must guard against two things which are apt to obscure it.

One is ignorance, which darkens it and impedes it in acquiring the knowledge of truth, the proper object of the understanding. Therefore it must be made clear and bright by exercise, that so it may be able to see and discern plainly all that is needful to purify the soul from disorderly passions, and to adorn it with saintly virtues.

This light may be obtained in two ways. The first and most important is prayer, imploring the Holy Ghost to pour it into our hearts. This He will not fail to do, if we in truth seek God alone and the fulfillment of His holy will, and if in all things we submit our Judgment to that of our spiritual father.

The other is, to exercise ourselves continually in a true and deep consideration of all things, to discover whether they be good or evil, according to the teaching of the Holy Ghost, and not according to their outward appearance, as they impress the senses or are judged of by the world.

This consideration, if rightly exercised will teach us to regard as falsehood and vanity all which the blind and corrupt world in so many various ways loves, desires, and seeks after. It will show us plainly that the honors and pleasures of earth are but vanity and vexation of spirit; that injury and infamy inflicted on us by the world bring true glory, and tribulations contentment; that to pardon our enemies and to do them good is true magnanimity, and an act which likens us most nearly to God; that to despise the world is better than to rule it; that voluntary obedience for the love of God to the meanest of His creatures is greater and nobler than to command mighty princes; and that the mortification and subjugation of our most trifling appetite is more glorious than the reduction of strong cities, the defeat of mighty armies, the working of miracles, or the raising of the dead.

VIII: Of the hindrances to a Right Discernment of Things, and of the method to be adopted in order to understand them properly

The cause of our not rightly discerning all these things and many others is, that we conceive a love or hatred of them at first sight. Our understanding is thus darkened, so that it cannot judge of them correctly.

Lest you fall into this delusion, take all possible care to keep your will pure and free from inordinate affection for anything whatsoever.

When any object, then, is presented to you, view it with your understanding; and consider it maturely before you are moved by hatred to reject it, if it be a thing contrary to your inclinations, or by love to desire it, if it be pleasing to them.

For thus the understanding, being unclouded by passion, will be free and clear, and able to perceive the truth, and to discern the evil which lurks behind delusive pleasure and the good which is veiled under the appearance of evil.

But if the will be first inclined to love or hate anything, the understanding will be unable to exercise a right judgment upon it. For the affection which has thus intruded itself so obscures the understanding, that it views the object as other than it is, and by thus representing it to the will, influences that faculty, in contradiction to every law and rule of reason, to love or hate it inordinately. The understanding is gradually darkened more and more, and in this deepening obscurity the object appears more and more hateful or lovely to the will.

Hence, if this most important rule be not observed, these two faculties, the understanding and the will, noble and excellent as they are, will soon sink in a miserable descent from darkness into thicker darkness, and from error into deeper error.

Guard yourself most vigilantly, then, from all inordinate affection for anything whatever, until you have first tested it by the light of the understanding, and chiefly by that of grace and prayer, and by the judgment of your spiritual father.

And this is to be observed most carefully with regard to such outward works as are good and holy, because the danger is greatest here of delusion and indiscretion.

Hence you may here receive serious injury from some circumstance of time, or place, or degree, or regarding obedience; as has been proved by many, who have incurred great danger in the performance of commendable and holy exercises.

IX: Of another danger from which the Understanding must be guarded in order that it may exercise a True Discernment

The second thing from which the understanding must be guarded is curiosity; for by filling it with hurtful, vain, and impertinent thoughts we incapacitate and disable it from apprehending that which most nearly affects our true mortification and perfection. To this end, you must be as one dead to all needless investigation of even lawful earthly things.

Always restrain your intellect as much as possible, and love to keep it low.

Let the news and the changes of the world, whether great or small, be to you as though, they were not; and should they intrude themselves, reject, and drive them from you.

Be sober and humble even in the desire to understand heavenly things, wishing to know nothing but Christ crucified, His life, His death, and what He requires of thee. Cast all other things far from you, and so shall you be very pleasing unto God. For He loves and delights in those who desire and seek of Him such things alone as serve to the love of His divine goodness and the fulfillment of His will. All other petitions and inquiries belong to self-love, pride, and the snares of the devil.

By following these instructions you will avoid many dangers; for when the wily serpent sees the will of those who are aiming at the spiritual life to be strong and resolute, he attacks their understanding, that so he may master both the one and the other.

He often, therefore, infuses lofty and curious speculations into their minds, especially if they be of an acute and intellectual order, and easily inflated with pride; and he does this in order that they may busy themselves in the enjoyment and discussion of such subjects, wherein, as they falsely persuade themselves, they enjoy God, and meanwhile neglect to purify their hearts and to apply themselves to self-knowledge and true mortification. So, falling into the snare of pride, they make an idol of their own understanding.

Hence, being already accustomed to have recourse in all circumstances to their own judgment, they come gradually and imperceptibly to believe that they have no need of advice or control from others.

This is a most perilous case, and very hard to cure, the pride of the understanding being more dangerous than that of the will; for when the pride of the will is once perceived by the understanding, it may in course of time be easily remedied by submission to those to whom it owes obedience. But how, or by whom, can he be cured, who obstinately believes his own opinion to be worth more than that of others? How shall he submit to other men's judgment, which he accounts to be far inferior to his own!

The understanding is the eye of the soul, by which the wound of the proud will should be discovered and cleansed; if that eye, then, itself be weak and blind and swollen with pride, by whom shall it be healed?

And if the light become darkness, and the rule faulty, what will become of the rest?

Therefore resist this dangerous pride betimes, before it penetrates into the marrow of your bones.

Blunt the acuteness of your intellect, willingly submit your own opinion to that of others, become a fool for the love of God, and you shall be wiser than Solomon.

X: Of the Exercise of the Will, and the end to which all our actions, whether Interior or Exterior, should tend

Besides this necessary exercise of the understanding, you must so regulate your will that it may not be left to follow its own desires, but may be in all things conformed to the Divine pleasure.

And remember, that it is not enough only to strive after those things which are most pleasing to God; but you must so will them, and so do them, as moved thereto by Him, and with a view to please Him alone.

In this exercise of the will, even more than in that of the understanding, we shall meet with strong opposition from nature, which seeks itself and its own ease and pleasure in all things; but especially in such as are holy and spiritual. It delights itself in these, feeding greedily upon them as upon wholesome food.

As soon, therefore, as they are presented to us we look wistfully upon them, and desire them, not because such is the will of God, nor with the sole view to please Him, but for the sake of the satisfaction and benefit to be derived from willing those things which God wills.

This delusion is the more subtle from the very excellence of the thing desired. Hence, even in the desire after God Himself, we are exposed to the delusions of self-love, which often leads us to look more to our own interests, and to the benefits we expect from God, than to His will, which is, that we should love, and desire and obey Him for His own glory alone.

I will now show you a way to avoid this way, which would impede you in the path of perfection, and to accustom yourself to will and to do all things as moved by the Spirit of God, and with the pure intention of honoring and pleasing Him alone, Who desires to be the one End and Principle of our every word and action. When anything presents itself to you as if willed by God, do not permit yourself to will it till you have first raised your thoughts to Him to discover whether He wills you to will it, and because He so wills it, and to please Him alone.

Let your will, then, being thus moved and attracted by His, be impelled to will it because He wills it, and solely to please and honor Him.

In like manner, if you would refuse things which are contrary to God's will, refuse them not till you have first fixed the eye of your mind upon His divine will, Who wills that you should refuse them solely to please Him.

Know, however that the frauds and deceits of wily nature are but little suspected; for, ever secretly seeking self, it often leads us to fancy that our end and motive is to please God when in reality it is far otherwise.

Thus, when we choose or refuse any thing for our own interest and satisfaction, we often imagine that we are choosing or refusing it in the hope of pleasing, or in the fear of displeasing, God.

The true and effectual remedy for this delusion is purity of heart, which consists in this — which is indeed the aim and object of all this spiritual warfare — the putting off the old man, and the putting on the new.

And to this end, seeing you are full of self, take care in the beginning of every action to free yourself as much as possible from all admixture of anything which seems to be your own.

Choose nothing, do nothing, refuse nothing, unless you first feel yourself moved and drawn thereto by the pure and simple will of God.

If you do not always feel thus actuated in the inward workings of the mind, and in outward actions, which are but transient, you must be content to have this motive ever virtually present, always maintaining a pure intention to please your God alone in all things. But in actions of longer duration it is well not only to excite this motive within yourself at the beginning, but also to renew it frequently, and to keep it alive till the end. Otherwise you will be in danger of falling into another snare of our natural self-love, which, as it is always inclined to yield rather to self than to God, often causes us unconsciously, in the course of time to change our objects and our aims.

The servant of God who is not on his guard against this danger, often begins a work with the single thought of pleasing his Lord alone; but soon, gradually and almost imperceptibly, he be- gins to take such pleasure in his work, that he loses sight of the Divine Will and follows his own. He dwells so much on the satisfaction he feels in what he is doing, and on the honor and benefit to be derived therefrom, that should God Himself place any impediment in the way, either by sickness or accident or through the agency of man, he is immediately troubled and disquieted, and often falls to murmuring against the impediment, whatever it may be, or rather, against God Himself – a clear proof that his intention was not wholly from God, but sprang from an evil root and a corrupted source.

For he who acts only as moved by God, and with a view to please Him alone, desires not one thing above another. He wishes only to have what it pleases God he should have, and at the time and in the way which may be most agreeable to Him; and whether he have it or not, he is equally tranquil and content; because in either case he obtains his wish, and fulfills his

intention, which is nothing else but simply to please God.
Therefore recollect yourself seriously, and be careful always
to direct every action to this perfect end.

And although the bent of your natural disposition should
move you to do good through fear of the pains of hell or hope
of the joys of paradise, you may even here set before you, as
your ultimate end, the will and pleasure of God, Who is
pleased that you should enter into His kingdom and not into
hell. It is not in man fully to apprehend the force and virtue of
this motive; for the most insignificant action, done with a view
to please God alone, and for His sole glory, is (if we may so
speak) of infinitely greater value than many others of the greatest dignity and importance done without this motive. Hence a
single penny given to a poor man with the sole desire to please
His Divine Majesty, is more acceptable to God than the entire
renunciation of all earthly goods for any other end, even for
the attainment of the bliss of heaven; an end in itself not only
good, but supremely to be desired.

This exercise of doing all things with the single aim to please
God alone seems hard at first, but will become plain and easy
by practice, if, with the warmest affections of the heart, we desire God alone, and long for Him as our only and most perfect
good; Who deserves that all creatures should seek Him for
Himself, and serve Him and love Him above all things.

The deeper and more continual our meditations are upon
His infinite excellence, the more fervent and the more frequent
will be these exercises of the will; and we shall thus acquire
more easily and more speedily the habit of performing every
action from pure love to that gracious Lord, Who alone is worthy of our reverence and love.

Lastly, in order to the attainment of this divine motive, I
advise you to seek it of God by importunate prayer, and to
meditate frequently upon the innumerable benefits which He,
of His pure and disinterested love, has bestowed upon us.

XI: Of some considerations which may incline the Will to seek to please God in all things

Furthermore, to incline the will more readily to seek God's honor and glory in all things, always remember that, in many and various ways, He has first loved and honored you.

In creation, by creating you out of nothing after His likeness, and all other creatures for your service.

In Redemption, by sending, not an angel, but His only begotten Son, to redeem you, not with the corruptible price of silver and gold, but with His Precious Blood, and by His most painful and ignominious death. Remember, that every hour, nay, every moment, He protects you from your enemies, fights for you by His grace, offers you continually, in the Sacrament of the Altar, His well-beloved Son, to be your food and your defense; are not all these tokens of the inestimable regard and love borne to you by the Infinite God? It is not in man to conceive, on the one hand, how great is the value which so great a Lord sets upon us poor creatures in our loneliness and misery; and, on the other, how great the return we are bound to make to His Supreme Majesty, Who has done so many and such great things for us.

For if earthly lords, when honored even by poor and lowly men, feel bound to honor them in return, how should our vile nature demean itself towards the Supreme King of heaven and earth, by Whom we are so dearly loved and so highly prized?

And besides all this, and before all things, keep ever vividly in mind that the Divine Majesty is infinitely worthy to be loved for Himself alone, and to be served purely for His own good pleasure.

XII: Of the diverse wills in Man, and the Warfare between them

Although in this combat we may be said to have within us two wills, the one of the reason which is called rational and superior, the other of the senses, called sensual and inferior, and commonly described by the words appetite, flesh, sense, and passion; yet, as it is the reason which constitutes us men, we cannot be said to will anything which is willed by the senses unless we be also inclined thereto by the superior will. And herein does our spiritual conflict principally consist. The reasonable will being placed, as it were, midway between the Divine will, which is above it - and the inferior will, or will of the senses, which is beneath it, is continually assaulted by both; each seeking in turn to attract and subdue, and bring it into obedience.

Much hard toil and trouble must, however, be undergone by the unpracticed, especially at the outset, when they resolve to amend their evil lives, and, renouncing the world and the flesh, to give themselves up to the love and service of Jesus Christ. For the opposition encountered by the superior will, from the continual warfare between the Divine and sensual will, is sharp and severe, and accompanied by acute suffering.

It is not so with those who are well practiced in the way of virtue or of vice; they pursue without difficulty the path on which they have entered; the virtuous yielding readily to the Divine will, and the vicious yielding without resistance to the will of the senses.

But let no one imagine it possible to persevere in the exercise of true Christian virtues, or to serve God as He ought to be served, unless he will in good earnest do violence to himself, and endure the pain of parting with all pleasant things whatsoever, whether great or small, around which his earthly affections are entwined.

Hence it is that so few attain to perfection; for after having with much toil overcome the greater vices, they will not persevere in doing violence to themselves by struggling against the promptings of self-will, and an infinity of lesser desires. They grow weary of so unremitting a struggle; they suffer these insignificant enemies to prevail against them, and so to acquire an absolute mastery over their hearts.

To this class belong men who, if they do not take what belongs to others, cleave with inordinate affection to that which is lawfully their own. If they do not obtain honors by unlawful means, yet they do not, as they should, shun them; but, on the contrary, cease not to desire, and sometimes even to seek, them in various ways. If they observe fasts of obligation, yet they do not mortify their palate in the matter of superfluous eating, or the indulgence in delicate morsels. If they live continently, yet they do not renounce many indulgences which much impede union with God and the growth of the spiritual life; and which, as they are very dangerous even to the holiest persons, and most dangerous to those who fear them least, should be as much as possible avoided by all.

Hence all their good works are performed in a lukewarm spirit, and accompanied by much self-seeking, by many lurking imperfections, by a certain kind of self-esteem, and by a desire to be praised and valued by the world.

Such persons not only fail to make any progress in the way of salvation, but rather go back; and are therefore in danger of relapsing into their former sins, because they have no love of true holiness, and show little gratitude to their Lord, Who rescued them from the tyranny of the devil. They are moreover too blind and ignorant to see the peril in which they stand; and so falsely persuade themselves of their own security.

And here we discover a delusion, which is the more dangerous because it is little apprehended. Many who aspire to the spiritual life, unconsciously love themselves far more than they ought to do; and therefore practice for the most part those exercises which suit their taste, and neglect others, which touch to the quick those natural inclinations and sensual appetites against which they ought in all reason to direct the full strength of the battle.

Therefore I exhort and counsel you to be in love with pain and difficulty; for they will bring with them that which is the end and object of the whole struggle: victory over-self. The more deeply you shall be in love with the difficulties encountered by beginners in virtue and in war, the surer and the speedier shall be the victory; and if your love be to the difficulty and the toilsome struggle, rather than to the victory and the virtue to be attained, you shall the more speedily obtain all you desire.

XIII: Of the way to resist the impulses of sense, and of the acts to be performed by the will in order to acquire Habits of Virtue

Whenever your reasonable will is attacked by the will of sense on the one hand, and the Divine will on the other, each seeking to obtain the mastery over it, you must make use of various exercises, in order that the Divine will may always govern you.

- ❖ First, whenever you are assailed and buffeted by the impulses of sense, oppose a valiant resistance to them, so that the superior will may not consent.
- ❖ Secondly, when the assaults have ceased, excite them anew, in order to repress them with greater force and vigor. Then challenge them again to a third conflict, wherein you may accustom yourself to repulse them with contempt and abhorrence. These two challenges to battle should be made to every disorderly appetite, except in the case of temptations of the flesh, concerning which we shall speak in their place.
- ❖ Lastly, make acts contrary to each evil passion which is to be resisted.

This will be made clear by the following example.

Suppose you are assailed by feelings of impatience. Look carefully into yourself, and you will find that these feelings are constantly directed against the superior will, in order to win its consent.

Now, then, begin the first exercise; and by repeated acts of the will, do all in your power to stifle each feeling as it arises, that your will may not consent to it. And never desist from this till, wearied unto death, your enemy yield himself vanquished.

But see here the malice of the devil. When he perceives that we resist the first movements of any passion, not only does he desist from exciting them, but when excited, he endeavors for the time to allay them, lest, by the exercise of resistance to the passion, we should acquire the habit of the opposite virtue. He would fain also betray us into the snares of pride and vainglory, by subtly insinuating to us that, like valiant soldiers, we have quickly trampled down our enemies.

Proceed, therefore, to the second conflict, recalling and exciting within yourself those thoughts which tempted you to impatience, until they sensibly affect you. Then set yourself to repress every such feeling with a stronger will and more earnest endeavor than before.

And because, however strenuously we have resisted our enemies, from a sense of duty and a desire to please God, we are still in danger, unless we hold them in perfect detestation, of being one day overcome, attack them again even a third time; and repel them, not with repugnance only, but with indignation, until they have become hateful and abominable in your sight.

Lastly, to adorn and perfect your soul in the habit of all the virtues, exercise yourself in the inward sets directly opposed to all your disorderly passions.

Would you attain, for instance, to the perfection of patience? On receiving any insult which tempts you to impatience, it will not be enough to exercise yourself in the three modes of warfare above described, you must do more even willingly accept and love the indignity you have endured; desiring to submit to it again, from the same person, and in the same manner; expecting and disposing yourself to bear still harder things.

These contrary acts are needful to our perfection in all the virtues, because the exercises of which we have been speaking - manifold and efficacious as they are - will not suffice to eradicate the roots of sin.

Hence (to pursue the same example) although, when we receive an insult, we do not yield to the impulse of impatience, but, on the contrary, resist it by the three methods above described, yet, unless we accustom ourselves by many and repeated acts of the will to love contempt, and rejoice to be despised, we shall never overcome the sin of impatience, which springs from a regard for our own reputation and a shrinking from contempt.

And if the vicious root be left alive, it is ever springing up afresh; causing virtue to languish, and sometimes to perish utterly, and keeping us in continual danger of relapse upon the first opportunity which may present itself. Without these contrary acts, therefore, we shall never acquire a true habit of virtue.

And bear in mind also, that these acts should be so frequent and so numerous, as utterly to destroy the vicious habit, which, as it had obtained possession of our heart by repeated acts of sin, so by contrary acts must it be dislodged, to make way for the habit of virtue.

Again, a greater number of virtuous acts is requisite to form the habit of virtue than of evil ones to form the habit of vice; because the former are not, like the latter, assisted by our corrupt nature.

I would add to all that has been said, that if the virtue in which you are exercising yourself so require, you must also practice exterior acts conformable to the interior; as, for instance, words of love and meekness, and lowly services rendered to those who have in any way thwarted or slighted you.

And though all these acts, whether interior or exterior, should be, or should seem to you to be, feebly and faintly done, and, as it were, against your will, yet you must not on any account neglect them; for feeble as they may be, they will keep you safe and steadfast in the fight, and smooth before you the path to victory.

And stand always prepared and on your guard to resist the

assaults of every passion, not only such as are violent and imperious, but the slightest and the gentlest; for these but open the way to the greater, by which habits of vice are gradually formed within us.

It has often happened, in consequence of the little care taken by some men to eradicate these lesser desires from their hearts, after they have overcome the more violent assaults of the same passion, that, when they have least expected it, their old enemies have fallen upon them again, and they have sustained a more complete and fatal defeat than had ever befallen them before.

Remember, again, to mortify and thwart your own wishes from time to time in lawful but not necessary things; for many benefits follow such discipline; it will prepare and dispose you more and more for self-mastery in other things; you will thus become expert and strong in the struggle with temptation; you will escape many a snare of the devil, and accomplish a work well pleasing to the Lord.

I speak plainly to you; if, in the way I have taught you, you will persevere faithfully in these holy exercises for self-reformation and self-mastery, I promise you that in a short time you will make great progress, and will become spiritual, not in name only, but in truth. But in no other manner do I bid you hope to attain to true holiness and spirituality, nor by any other exercises, however excellent in your estimation, though you should seem to be wholly absorbed in them, and to hold sweet colloquies with our Lord.

For, as I told you in the first chapter, true holiness and spirituality consists not in exercises which are pleasing to us and conformable to our nature, nor is it produced by these, but by such only as nail that nature, with all its works, to the cross, and, renewing the whole man by the practice of the evangelical virtues, unite him to his crucified Savior and Creator.

There can be no question that as habits of vice are formed by many and frequent acts of the superior will yielding itself to the sway of the sensual appetites, so, on the contrary, habits of evangelical virtue are acquired by the performance of frequent and repeated acts of conformity to the Divine Will, Which calls upon us to exercise ourselves now in one virtue, now in another.

For as our will, however fiercely assailed by sin or by the suggestions of our lower nature, can never become sinful or earthly unless it yield or incline itself to the temptation, so you will never attain to holiness and union with God, however powerfully called and mightily assailed by Divine grace and heavenly inspirations, unless by inward, and, if need be, by outward acts, your will be made conformable to His.

XIV: What must be done when the superior-will seems to be wholly stifled and overcome by the interim-will and by other enemies

If at times the superior will should seem to you powerless to resist the inferior and its other enemies because you do not feel within you an effectual will opposed to them, yet stand firm, and do not quit the field; for you must always account yourself victorious until you can clearly perceive that you have yielded.

For inasmuch as our superior will has no need of the inferior for the production of its acts, without its own consent it can never be compelled to yield, however sorely assaulted.

For God endued our will with such freedom and such strength, that were all the senses, all evil spirits, nay, the whole world itself, to arm and conspire to assault and oppress it with all their might, it could still, in spite of them, will or not will all that it wills or wills not; and that how often so-ever, when-so-ever, how-so-ever, and to what end so-ever it should please.

And if at any time your foes should so violently assail and press upon you as almost to stifle your will, so that it seems to have no breath to produce any opposing act of volition, yet do not lose courage, nor throw down your arms, but make use of your tongue in your defense, saying, "I yield not, I consent not;" like a man whose adversary is upon him and holds him down, and who, being unable to reach him with the point of his sword, strikes at him with the hilt; and as he tries to make a spring backwards to wound his enemy with the point, so do thou take refuge in the knowledge of yourself, the knowledge that you are nothing, and can do nothing, and with faith in God, Who can do all things, strike a blow at this hostile passion, saying: "Help me, Lord! help me, O my God! help me, Jesus, Mary! that I may not yield to this enemy."

You may also, when your enemy gives you time, call in your reason to assist the weakness of your will, by meditating upon various points, the consideration of which may give it strength and restore its breath to resist the enemy. For example: You are, perhaps, under some persecution or other trial, so sorely tempted to impatience, that your will, as it seems to you, cannot, or at least will not, endure it. Encourage it, then, by discussing with the reason such points as the following:

- ❖ Consider, first, whether you have given any occasion for the evil under which you are suffering and so have deserved it; for if you have done so, every rule of justice requires of you to bear patiently the wound which with your own hand you have inflicted on yourself.

- ❖ Second, if blameless in this particular instance think of your other sins, for which God has not yet chastised you, and for which you have not, as you should have done, duly punished yourself. Seeing, then, that God's mercy changes your deserved punishment, which should be eternal, into some light affliction which is but temporal, you should receive it, not willingly only, but thankfully.

- ❖ Third, should your offenses against the Divine Majesty seem to you to be light, and the penance you have endured for them heavy (a persuasion, however, which you should never allow yourself to entertain), you must remember that it is only through the straight gate of tribulation that you can enter into the kingdom of heaven.

❖ Fourth, that even were it possible to enter there by any other way, the law of love forbids you so much as to think of it, seeing that the Son of God, with all His friends and all His members, entered into that kingdom by a path strewed with thorns and crosses.

❖ Fifth, that which you have chiefly to consider, on this and all other occasions, is the will of God, Who, for the love He bears you, views with unspeakable complacency every act of virtue and mortification which, as His faithful and valiant soldier, you perform in requital of His love to you. And of this be assured, that the more unreasonable in itself the trial seems, and the more ignominious, by reason of the unworthiness of those from whom it comes, and so the more vexatious and the harder to be borne, so much the more pleasing will you be to the Lord, if in things so disordered in themselves, and therefore so bitter and repugnant to you, you can approve and love His Divine Will and Providence, in which all events, however adverse, are disposed after a most perfect rule and order.

XV: Some advice touching the manner of this warfare, and especially against whom, and with what resolution, it must be carried on

You see now after what manner you must fight in order to conquer self, and to adorn your soul with all virtues. Know, furthermore, that to obtain a speedier and easier victory over your enemies, it is expedient, nay necessary, that you should fight against them daily, and especially against self-love, and learn to esteem as dear friends and benefactors all the insults and vexatious which the world can heap upon you.

And it is because men know not the necessity of this daily warfare, and make too little account of it, that, as I said before, their victories are rare, difficult, imperfect, and unstable.

Moreover, I warn you that you must bring great steadfastness of soul to this conflict. And this gift you will readily obtain if you beseech it of God; considering, on the one hand, the undying hatred and fury of your enemies, and the vast multitude of their ranks and squadrons; and, on the other, how infinitely greater is the goodness of God and the love wherewith He loves you, and how much mightier, too, are the angels of heaven, and the prayers of the saints, which fight for us.

By this consideration have so many feeble women been enabled to overcome and conquer all the power and wisdom of the world, all the assaults of the flesh, and all the fury of hell.

Therefore you must never be dismayed, though at times your enemy seem to be strengthening his array against you, though the struggle threaten to last your whole lifetime and though al- most certain falls menace you on every side; for know assuredly, that the whole strength and wisdom of our enemies is in the hands of our Divine Captain, in whose honor the battle is arrayed; Who, prizing us beyond measure, sure, and having Himself imperatively called us to the conflict, will never suffer you to be overcome. Nay more, He will Himself fight on your right hand, and will not fail in His own good time to subdue your foes before you; and this to your greater reward, if He should delay to give you the victory till the last day of your life.

This alone is your concern, to fight manfully, and never, however numerous your wounds, to lay down your arms or take to flight.

Lastly, that you fail not to fight courageously bear in mind that this is a conflict whence there is no escape; and that he who will not fight must needs be captured or slain. Moreover, we have to deal with enemies so powerful, and go filled with deadly hate, as to leave us no hope of either peace or truce.

XVI: In what manner the soldier-of-Christ should take the field early in the morning

"**N**ot by might nor by power, but by my Spirit," says the Lord Almighty (Zechariah 4:6).

On awaking in the morning, the first thing to be observed by your inward sight is the listed field in which you are enclosed, the law of the combat being that he who fights not must there lie dead forever. Here picture to yourself, on one side, your enemy (that evil inclination which you are already pledged to conquer) now standing before you, ready armed to wound and slay you; see also, on the right hand, your victorious Captain Jesus Christ, with His most holy Mother the Virgin Mary, and her beloved spouse Saint Joseph, and innumerable hosts of angels, especially Saint Michael the archangel; and, on the left hand, the infernal demon, with all his armies, ready to excite this passion and to persuade you to yield to it. Then shall you seem to hear a voice as of your guardian angel addressing you:

> "You are to fight this day against this and other enemies of yours. Let not your heart fail, nor your spirit faint. Yield not on any account, neither for fear nor any other cause; for our Lord, your Leader, stands beside you with all His glorious hosts, and will do battle for you against all your enemies and will not suffer their form to prevail against you or to overcome you."

> "Only stand firm; do violence to yourself, and endure the pain such violence will cause you. Cry unceasingly from the depths of your heart, and call upon the Lord, and so assuredly shalt you gain the victory. If you are weak and inexperienced, if your enemies are strong and manifold, manifold more are the succors of Him Who created and redeemed you, and mightier beyond all measure and comparison is your God, and more willing to save you than are all your

enemies to destroy you."

"Fight valiantly then, and be not loathe to suffer; for it is this toilsome resistance to your evil inclinations, this painful struggle against evil habits, which shall gain you the victory, and win for you a treasure wherewith to purchase the kingdom of heaven, and unite your soul to God forever."

Begin the combat in the name of the Lord, with the weapons of self-distrust and trust in God, of prayer and spiritual exercises; and challenge to the battle your foe, that is, that inclination, whatever it be, which, according to the order above laid down, you have resolved to conquer. Do this, now by open resistance, now by deep abhorrence, or, again, by acts of the contrary virtue, wounding him again and again, even unto death, to give plea- sure to your Lord, Who is looking on, with the whole Church triumphant, to behold your conflict.

I tell you again, you must not weary of the struggle, but remember the obligation which lies on us all to serve and please God, and the absolute necessity of fighting in this battle, from which none can escape without wounds or death. I tell you, moreover, that if as a rebel you would fly from God, and give yourself over to the world and the delights of the flesh, you will still be forced, in spite of yourself, to labor in the sweat of your brow against many and many an adversary, who will pierce your heart with deadly anguish.

Consider, then, what folly it would be to incur all this toil and trouble, which does but lead to greater toil, and endless trouble and spiritual death, in order to avoid that which will soon be over, and which will lead us to eternal and infinite blessedness in the everlasting enjoyment of our God.

XVII: Of the order to be observed in the conflict with our Evil Passions

It is of great importance that we should know how to observe a due order in this combat, lest, as too many do to their own great injury, we should fight in a casual or desultory manner. The order to be observed in the warfare against your enemies and evil inclinations should be as follows:

Look well into your heart, and search diligently till you have discovered by what thoughts and affections it is surrounded, and by what passion it is most tyrannously swayed; and against this first take up arms and direct your attack. If meanwhile you should be assaulted by other enemies, turn against the one nearest to you and which at the moment threatens you; but fail not to return afterwards to the prosecution of your principal enterprise.

XVIII: Of the way to resist sudden impulses of the Passions

Until we have become habituated toward our sudden strokes, whether of insult or other adverse circumstances, it is well, in order to acquire such a habit, to anticipate them, and desire to suffer them over and over again, and so to await them with a mind prepared.

The way to anticipate them is, to consider the passion to which you are most inclined, and also the places wherein and the persons with whom you are wont to converse; whence you may readily conjecture what is likely to befall you. And should you meet with any other untoward circumstance which you have not foreseen, although you will find your soul strengthened by having been prepared to meet the other evils which you did foresee, yet may you also avail yourself of the following additional help.

At the very first touch of the insult or "trial", whatever it be, rouse yourself at once, and lift up your heart to God, reflecting on His ineffable goodness and love, which sends you this affliction, that, by enduring it for the love of Him, you may thereby be more purified, and brought nearer and united unto Him.

And, knowing how greatly He is pleased that you should suffer it, turn next to yourself and with a sharp rebuke say, "O, why will you refuse to bear this cross, which is sent to you not by man, but by your Father Who is in heaven!" Then turn to the cross, and embrace it with all possible patience and joy, saying, "O cross, formed by Divine providence before I was born; O cross, endeared to me by the dear love of my crucified Lord, nail me now to you, that so I may give myself to Him Who died on you for my redemption!"

And if at first the passion should prevail against you, and you should be wounded, and unable to raise your heart to God, strive even then to do as at the beginning, and fight as if still unwounded.

The most effectual remedy, however, against these sudden impulses is to remove the cause from whence they proceed. Thus, if you discover that, through your affection for any object, you are thrown into a sudden agitation of mind as often as it is presented to you, the remedy is by persevering efforts to withdraw your affection from it.

But if the agitation proceed from a person who is so disagreeable to you that every little action of his annoys and irritates you, the remedy here is to force yourself to love and cherish him, not only as a creature formed by the same sovereign Hand with yourself, and created anew by the same Divine Blood, but also because he offers you an opportunity, if you will accept it, of becoming like your Lord, Who is kind and loving unto all men.

XIX: Of the way to resist the sins of the Flesh

These sins must be resisted in a way peculiar to themselves, and different from the method used against any other temptation.

In order, therefore, to a successful resistance, three periods must be observed.

- ❖ Before the temptation,
- ❖ During the temptation, and
- ❖ After the temptation.

Before the temptation the struggle must be against those things which generally occasion it.

First, you must combat the vice, but never confront it; on the contrary, avoid to the utmost of your power every occasion and every person where you may incur the slightest danger. And if at times compelled to converse with such, let it be briefly, with a grave and modest demeanor, and with worlds of severity rather than of excessive tenderness and ability.

Neither be confident in yourself if you are free, and during many years of such exercises have continued free from temptations of the flesh; for this accursed vice makes its advances secretly, often doing in an hour what in many years it had failed to effect; and it hurts the more grievously, and wounds the more fatally, the more friendly the form it assumes, and the less ground of suspicion it seems to give.

And there is often great danger, as experience has shown and still shows, in intercourse which is indulged in under fair and lawful pretexts, such as kindred, relations of duty, or, again, great virtue in the person beloved. For the poisonous pleasure of sense insinuates itself into this over-frequent and imprudent intercourse, instilling its venom gradually, until it penetrates into the marrow of the soul and darkens the reason more and more, till at last no account is made of things which are really dangerous, such as mutual glances of tenderness, loving words, and the enjoyment of conversation; and so, a change creeping over both, they fall at last into destruction, or into some temptation most hard and toilsome to overcome.

Once more I say to you, Fly! for you are as stubble. Trust not to being bathed and filled with the water of a good and strong purpose, and resolved and ready to die rather than o end God; for, inflamed by frequent stirring the heat of the re will gradually dry up the water of thy good resolve, and when you are least on your guard, it will so enkindle you that you will respect neither friends nor kindred, nor fear God, nor regard life or honor nor all the pains of hell. Therefore fly, fly unless you would be overtaken, captured, and slain.

Secondly, avoid idleness, and be awake and vigilant, and busied with the thoughts and deeds which benefit your state of life.

Thirdly, never resist the will of your superiors; but show them a ready obedience, fulfilling promptly all their commands, and most willingly such as humble you most, and are most opposed to your natural will and inclination.

Fourthly, beware of forming rash judgments of your neighbor, especially with regard to this vice; and if he have manifestly fallen, have pity on him; be not bitter against him, nor hold him in contempt; but rather gather from his fall the fruit of humility and self-knowledge, confessing yourself to be but dust and ashes, drawing nearer unto God in prayer, and shunning more carefully than ever all intercourse wherein there may be even the shadow of danger.

For if you are forward to judge and despise others, God will correct you to your cost, and suffer you to fall into the same fault in order to convince you of your weakness, that by such a humiliation both sins may be cured.

And even if you should escape this sin yet, unless you lay aside your uncharitable judgment of others, your state will be very insecure.

Fifthly and lastly, beware, lest, finding yourself favored with some enjoyment of spiritual delights, you feel a certain vain complacency therein, and imagine yourself to be something, and that your enemies are now no longer able to assault you, because you seem to yourself to regard them with disgust, horror, and detestation. If you are incautious in this matter, you will easily fall.

During the temptation, consider whether it proceeds from internal or external causes.

By external, I mean curiosity of the eyes or ears, over-softness in dress, habits, and conversations, which excite to this sin.

The remedies in this case are purity, modesty, the refraining from seeing or hearing anything which excites to this vice, and, as I said before, flight.

The internal are either the rebellion of the flesh, or thoughts of the mind proceeding from our own evil habits or from the suggestion of the devil.

The rebellion of the flesh must be mortified by fasts, disciplines, hair-shirts, vigils, and other similar austerities, as discretion and obedience may direct.

Against evil thoughts, from whatever source arising, the remedies are as follows:

❖ Occupation in the various duties proper to our state of life.

❖ Prayer and meditation.

Prayer should be made in the following manner:

When first conscious of the presence of these evil thoughts, or even of such as may betoken their approach, fly for refuge at once to the Crucifix, saying: "My Jesus! My sweet Jesus! Help me speedily, that I may not fall into the hands of this enemy."

And sometimes, embracing the cross on which your Lord is extended, and kissing repeatedly the wounds of His sacred feet, say lovingly: "O beauteous wounds! Chaste wounds! Holy wounds! Wound now this miserable impure heart of mine, and free it from all that offends Thee."

At the moment when temptations to carnal pleasures assail you, I do not advise you to meditate upon certain points recommended in many books as remedies against these temptations, such as the vileness of this vice, its insatiable craving, the bitterness and loathing, the peril and ruin of estate, life, honor, etc. which follow in its train.

This is not always a certain method of overcoming the temptation; for if the mind repels these thoughts on the one hand, on the other they afford an opportunity, and expose us to the danger of taking pleasure in, and consenting to, them. Therefore the true remedy in all these cases is flight, not from these thoughts alone, but from everything, however contrary to them, which may bring them before us.

Let your meditation, then, for this end be on the Life and Passion of our crucified Redeemer.

And should the same thoughts again intrude themselves against your will, and molest you more than ever, as will very probably happen, be not discouraged on this account, nor leave off your meditation, but continue it with all possible intensity; not even turning from it to repel such thoughts, but giving yourself no more concern about them than if they in no way belonged to you. There is no better method than this of resisting them, how incessant so-ever may be their attacks.

You will then conclude your meditation with this or some similar supplication: "Deliver me, O my Creator and Redeemer, from mine enemies, to the honor of Thy Passion and of Thine unspeakable goodness." Suffer not your thoughts to recur again to the subject; for the bare recollection of it is not without danger.

Neither stay at any time to reason with such temptations, to find out whether you have consented to them or not; for this is a device of the devil, who seeks, under the semblance of good, to disquiet you, and make you distrustful and faint-hearted, or hopes, by entangling you in such discussions, to draw you into some sin.

Therefore, in this temptation, when the consent is not evident, it is sufficient that you confess the whole briefly to your spiritual father, and then rest satisfied with his opinion, without thinking of it more

But be sure faithfully to reveal every thought to him; and neither be restrained from so doing by shame or any other consideration.

For if, in dealing with all our enemies, we need the grace of humility to enable us to subdue them, in this case more than in any other we are bound to humble ourselves; this vice being almost always the punishment of pride.

When the temptation is over, however free, however perfectly secure you may feel yourself from danger, keep far from all those objects which gave rise to the temptation, even though you should be induced to do otherwise for some apparently good and useful end. This is a deception of our evil nature, and a snare of our cunning adversary, who transforms himself into an angel of light to bring us into darkness.

XX: How to combat Sloth

To avoid falling into the miserable bondage of sloth, which would not only hinder your progress towards perfection, but also deliver you into the hands of your enemies, you must observe the fol- lowing rules:

1. Shun all curiosity concerning worldly things and all attachment to them, and also every kind of occupation which belongs not to your state of life.

2. Endeavor earnestly to respond immediately to every inspiration from above, and to every command of your superiors; doing everything at the time and in the manner which is pleasing to them.

3. Never allow yourself in one moment's delay; for that one little delay will soon be followed by another, and that by a third, and this again by others; and to the last the senses will yield and give way more easily than to the first, having been already fascinated and enslaved by the pleasure they have tasted therein.

Hence the duty to be performed is either begun too late, or sometimes laid aside altogether, as too irksome to be endured.

Thus, by degrees, a habit of sloth is acquired, which, as we cannot disguise it from ourselves, we seek to excuse by vain purposes of future diligence and activity, while we are all the time held in bondage by it.

The poison of sloth overspreads the whole man; not only infecting the will, by making exertion hateful to it, but also blinding the understanding, so that it is unable to see how vain and baseless are its intentions to do promptly and diligently at some future season what should be done at once, but is either willfully neglected altogether or deferred to another time.

Nor is it enough that we perform our appointed work quickly; we must, in order to bring it to its highest possible perfection, do it at the very time required by its nature and quality, and with all suitable diligence.

For that is not diligence, but the subtlest form of sloth, which leads us to do our work before its time; not seeking to do it well, but dispatching it hastily, that we may afterwards indulge in the sluggish repose on which our thoughts have been dwelling while we were hurrying over our business.

All this great evil proceeds from the want of duly considering the value of a good work performed at its right time, and with a spirit determined to brave the toil and difficulty put in the way of untried soldiers by the sin of sloth.

Call to mind, then, frequently, that a single elevation of the heart to God, a single genuflection in His honor, is worth more than all the treasures of the world; and that, as often as we do violence to ourselves and our sinful passions, a glorious crown of victory is prepared for us by angels' hands in the kingdom of heaven.

Remember also, on the other hand, that God gradually draws from the slothful the grace which He had once bestowed upon them; while He increases that of the diligent, permitting them at last to enter into His joy.

If you are unequal at first to a bold encounter with toil and hardship, disguise them from yourself, that they may not seem so formidable as sloth would represent them.

The exercise before you is perhaps to acquire some virtue by many repeated acts, by many days of toil; and the enemies to be overcome seem to you many and strong. Begin these acts, then, as if you had but a few of them to perform, but a few days' conflict to endure. Fight only against one adversary, as if there were no more to be resisted, and in full confidence that with the help of God, you will be stronger than they. By this means sloth will begin to grow feeble, and will make way at last for the gradual entrance of the contrary virtue.

I would say the same of prayer. An hour-prayer perhaps is needful for you; and this seems a hard matter to sloth; but apply yourself to it, as if intending to pray but for the eighth part of an hour, you will then easily pass on to another eighth; and so on to the whole.

But if in the second, or any other of these divisions you should feel too violent a repugnance and difficulty, leave the exercise awhile, lest you become weary; but return to, it shortly.

You should pursue the same method with respect to manual labors, when you are called upon to do things which to sloth appear many in number and di cult of performance, and so cause you much disturbance of mind. Begin, therefore, quietly and courageously with one, as if you had no more to do; and when you have diligently accomplished this, you will be able to perform all the others with far less labor than sloth would have you believe possible.

But if you do not pursue this method, and encounter resolutely the toil and hardships which lie in your way, the vice of sloth will so gain the mastery over you, that you will be forever harassed and annoyed, not only by the present toil and difficulty, which will always attend the first exercises of virtue, but even by the distant prospect of them. You will be forever in fear of being tried and assailed by enemies, or laden with some fresh burden; so that even in the time of peace you will live in perpetual disquiet.

Know, also, that this vice of sloth will not only consume by its secret poison the first and feeble roots, which would in time have produced habits of virtue, but even the roots of habits already acquired. Like a worm in the wood, it will go on insensibly corroding and eating away the marrow of the spiritual life.

By these means does the devil seek to ensnare and delude all men; but especially spiritual persons.

Watch, therefore, and pray, and labor diligently, and delay not to weave the web of your wedding-garment, that you may be found ready adorned to meet the Bridegroom.

And remember daily, that He Who gives you the morning does not promise you the evening; and though He gives the evening, yet promises not the morrow.

Spend, therefore, every moment of every hour according to God's will, as if it were your last; and so much the more carefully, as for every moment you will have to give the strictest account.

Finally, I warn you to account that day lost though it may have been full of busy action, in which you shall neither have gained some victory over your evil inclinations and your self-will, nor returned thanks to your Lord for His mercies, and especially for His bitter passion endured for you; and for His sweet and fatherly correction, when He has made you worthy to receive at His hand the inestimable treasure of suffering.

XXI: Of the regulation of the Exterior Senses, and how to pass on from these to the contemplation of the Divinity

Great watchfulness and continual exercise is needed for the due ordering and regulation of the exterior senses; for the appetite, which is, as it were, the captain of our corrupt nature, inclines us to an immoderate seeking after pleasure and enjoyment; and being unable by itself to attain them, it uses the senses as its soldiers, and as natural instruments for laying hold of objects whose images it draws to itself and impresses on the mind. Hence arises the pleasure, which, by reason of the relation subsisting between it and the flesh, di uses itself over all the senses which are capable of it, infecting both soul and body with a common contagion, which corrupts the whole.

You see the evil; now mark the remedy.

Take good heed not to let your senses stray freely where they will; nor to use them when pleasure alone, and not utility, necessity, nor any good end, is the motive. And if inadvertently they have been allowed to wander too far, recall them at once; or so regulate them, that, instead of remaining as before in a miserable captivity to empty pleasures, they may gather a noble spoil from each passing object, and bring it home to the soul, that, collected within herself, she may rise with a steadier flight towards heaven to the contemplation of God. This may be done in the following manner:

When any object is presented before one of your exterior senses, separate in your mind from the material thing the principle which is in it; and reflect that of itself it possesses nothing of all that which it appears to have, but that all is the work of God, Who endows it invisibly by His Spirit with the being, beauty, goodness, or whatever virtue belongs to it. Then rejoice that thy Lord alone is the Cause and Principle of such great and varied perfections, and that they are all eminently contained in Himself, all created excellences being but most minute degrees of His divine and infinite perfections. When engaged in the contemplation of grand and noble objects, reduce the creature mentally to its own nothingness; fixing your mind's eye on the great Creator therein present, who gave it that great and noble being, and delighting yourself in Him alone, say: "O Divine Essence, and above all things to be desired, how greatly do I rejoice that Thou alone are the infinite Principle of every created being!"

In like manner, at the sight of trees, plants, or suchlike objects, you will understand that the life which they have, they have not of themselves but from the Spirit which you do not see, and which alone quickens them. Say, therefore: "Behold here the true Life from which, in which, and by which all things live and grow! O living Joy of this heart!"

So, at the sight of brute animals, raise your thoughts to God, who gave them sensation and motion, saying: "O Thou first Mover of all that moves, Thou are Thyself immovable; how greatly do I rejoice in Thy steadfastness and stability!"

And if attracted by the beauty of the creature, separate that which you see from the Spirit which you see not, and consider that all that exterior beauty is solely derived from the invisible Spirit which is its source; and joyfully say: "Behold, these are streamlets from the uncreated Fountain; behold, these are drops from the infinite Ocean of all good. O, how does my inmost heart rejoice at the thought of that eternal infinite Beauty which is the source and origin of all created beauty!"

And on the discovery in other men of goodness, wisdom, justice, or similar virtues, make the same mental separation, and say to God: "O most rich Treasure-house of all virtues, how greatly do I rejoice that from Thee and through Thee alone flows all goodness, and that all in comparison with Thy Divine perfections is as nothing! I thank Thee, Lord, for this and every good gift which Thou hast vouchsafed to my neighbor; remember, Lord, my poverty, and my great need of this very virtue."

When you stretch out your hand to do anything, reflect that God is the first cause of that action, and you but His living instrument; and raising your thoughts to Him, say thus: "How great, O supreme Lord of all, is my interior joy, that without Thee I can do nothing, and that Thou are in truth the first and chief Worker of all things!"

When eating or drinking, consider that it is God who gives its relish to your food. Delighting yourself, therefore, in Him alone, say: "Rejoice, O my soul, that as there is no true contentment but in God, so in Him alone may you in all things content yourself."

When your senses are gratified by some sweet odor, rest not in this enjoyment, but let your thoughts pass on to the Lord, from Whom this sweetness is derived; and, inwardly consoled by this thought, say: "Grant, O Lord, that like as I rejoice because all sweetness flows from Thee, so may my soul, pure and free from all earthly pleasure, ascend on high as a sweet savor acceptable unto Thee."

When you listen to the harmony of sweet sounds, let your heart turn to God, saying: "How do I rejoice, my Lord and God, in Thine infinite perfections, which not only make a super-celestial harmony within Thyself, but also unite the angels in heaven and all created beings in one marvelous harmonious concert!"

XXII: How the same things are to us means where-by to regulate our senses, and to lead us on to meditate on the Incarnate Word in the Mysteries of His Life and Passion

I have shown you how we may raise our minds from sensible objects to the contemplation of the Divinity. Now learn a method of taking occasion from the same to meditate on the Incarnate Word, and the most sacred mysteries of His Life and Passion.

All things in the universe may serve to this end, if first you behold God in them as the sole first cause, Who has bestowed on them all the being, beauty, and excellence which they possess. Passing on from this, consider how great, how immeasurable is His goodness; Who, being the sole Principle and Lord of all creation, was pleased to descend so low as to become Incarnate, to suffer and to die for man, permitting the very works of His Hands to arm themselves against Him, and to crucify Him. Many objects will then bring these holy mysteries before your mind's eye, such as weapons, cords, scourges, pillars, thorns, reeds, nails, hammers, and other instruments of His Passion.

Poor hovels will recall to our memory the stable and manger of our Lord. Rain will remind us of the drops of Divine Blood which fell from His most sacred Body in the garden, and watered the ground. Rocks will represent to us those which were rent asunder at His death. The earth will bring to our memory the earthquake at that hour; the sun, the darkness that then covered it. The sight of water will speak to us of that stream which owed from His most Sacred Side.

The same may be said of other similar things.

- ❖ Let the taste of wine, or other liquid, remind you of your Lord's vinegar and gall.
- ❖ If sweet perfumes refresh you, think of the ill savior of the dead bodies which were around Him on Calvary.
- ❖ While dressing, recollect that the Eternal Word clothed Himself with human flesh that He might clothe you with His Divinity.
- ❖ When undressing, remember Christ, Who was stripped of His garments to be scourged and crucified for you.
- ❖ If you hear the shouts and cries of a multitude, think of those hateful words: "Away with Him, away with Him! crucify Him, crucify Him!" which sounded in His Divine Ears.
- ❖ At each stroke of the clock, think of that deep sorrow and heaviness of heart which Jesus was pleased to endure in the garden, as the fear of His approaching death and passion began to fall upon Him; or image to yourself those heavy blows which nailed Him to the Cross.
- ❖ On any occasion of grief or sorrow which presents itself, whether your own or another's, reflect that all these things are as nothing, compared to the inconceivable anguish which pierced and wrung the Soul and Body of thy Lord.

XXIII: Of some other means whereby we may regulate our senses according to the different occasions which present themselves

Having now seen by what means we may raise the mind from sensible objects to the contemplation of the Divinity and of the mysteries of the Incarnate Word, I will here add some helps for various subjects of meditation, that as the tastes of souls are many and various, so also may be their nourishment.

This may be awful, not only to simple persons, but also to those of higher intellect and more advanced in the spiritual life, who nevertheless may not at all times be equally disposed and ready for higher contemplations.

Nor need you fear to be perplexed by the variety of the methods described, if you will only observe the rule of discretion, and attend to the advice of others; which I wish you to follow with all humility and confidence, not in this instance only, but with regard to all other counsels which you shall receive from me.

❖ At the sight of all the things which please the eyes and are prized on earth, consider that all these are vile as dust compared with heavenly riches, after which, despising the whole earth, do you aspire with undivided affections.

❖ When looking upon the sun, consider that your soul is brighter and more beautiful if it be in your Creator's favor; if not, that it is blacker and more hateful than the darkness of hell.

❖ When your bodily eyes are lifted to the heavens above you, let the eyes of your mind penetrate even to the Heaven of heavens; and there fix yourself in thought as in the place prepared for your eternal and blessed abode, if you shall live a holy life on earth.

❖ On hearing the songs of birds, or other melodious sounds, lift up your heart to the songs of Paradise, where resounds a ceaseless Alleluia; and pray the Lord too make you worthy to praise Him together with those celestial spirits, for ever and ever. If you are conscious of taking delight in the beauty of the creature, remember that there the deadly serpent lies hid, ready and eager to wound, if not to slay you, and say to him: "O accursed serpent, you insidiously lie in wait to devour me!" Then turning to God, say: "Blessed be Thou, O my God, Who has discovered to me the hidden enemy, and delivered me from his ravenous jaws." Then fly at

once from the allurement to the wounds of your crucified Lord, letting your mind rest on them, considering
how acutely He suffered in His most Sacred Flesh to
free you from sin, and make you detest all carnal delights. Another way of escape from this perilous allurement is, to consider what will be, after death, the condition of that object which now so delights you.

❖ When walking, remember that every step brings you
nearer to death.

❖ Let the flight of birds and the owing of water remind
you that your life is hastening far more swiftly to its
close.

❖ Let storms of wind, lightning and thunder, remind you
of the tremendous day of judgment; and kneeling down,
worship God, and beseech Him to give you time and
grace duly to prepare yourself to appear before His
most high Majesty.

In the variety of accidents which may befall you, exercise
yourself thus:

❖ When, for instance, you are oppressed by sadness or
melancholy, or suffer heat, cold, or the like, lift up your
heart to that Eternal Will, Which for your own good
wills that at such a time and in such a measure you
should endure this discomfort. Then, rejoicing in the
love thus shown you by God, and at the opportunity of
serving Him in the way He is pleased to appoint, say in
your heart, "Behold in me is the Divine Will fulfilled,
Which from all eternity has lovingly appointed that I
should now endure this trial. All praise be to Thee for
the same, my most gracious Lord!"

❖ When any good thought arises in your mind, turn instantly to God, and, referring it to Him give thanks to
Him for it.

❖ When reading, behold your Lord in the words, and re
ceive them as from His Divine Lips.

- When you look upon the Holy Cross, consider that it is the standard of your warfare; that by forsaking it you will fall into the hands of cruel enemies, but that by following it you will enter heaven laden with glorious spoils.
- When you see the dear image of the Blessed Virgin Mary, let your heart turn to her who reigns in Paradise, thanking her that she was ever ready to do the will of God, that she brought forth and nourished the Redeemer of the world, and that her favor and assistance never fail us in our spiritual conflict.
- The images of the saints represent to you so many champions, who, having courageously run their course, have opened a way for you, wherein, if you will press onward, you also shall with them be crowned with immortal glory.
- When you see a church, you may, amid other devout reflections, consider that your soul is the temple of God, and therefore to be kept pure and spotless as His dwelling-place.
- When you hear the triple sound of the Angelus, make the following brief meditations in conformity with the words which are said before each recitation of the Ave Maria. At the first stroke of the bell, thank God for that embassy from heaven to earth which was the beginning of our salvation. At the second, rejoice with the blessed Mary at the sublime dignity to which she was exalted by her singular and most profound humility. At the third, adore, together with the most blessed Mother and the Angel Gabriel, the Divine Child just now conceived; and forget not reverently to bow your head at each signal, especially the last.

These meditations will serve for all seasons. The following, which are divided for morning, noon, and evening, belong to the Passion of our Lord, for we are deeply bound frequently to remember the sorrow endured by our Lady on this account, and most ungrateful were we to neglect it.

❖ In the evening then, recall to mind the anguish of that most pure Virgin at the bloody sweat, the capture, and the hidden sorrows of her blessed Son.

❖ In the morning, compassionate her affliction at His presentation before Pilate and Herod. His condemnation, and the bearing of His cross.

❖ At midday, meditate upon that sword of anguish which wounded the heart of that disconsolate Mother at the crucifixion and death of the Lord, and the cruel piercing of His most sacred side.

These meditations on our Lady's sorrows may be made from the evening of Thursday till the Saturday at noon, the others on the remaining days of the week. I leave all this, however, to your particular devotion and the occasions offered by external things; and, to express in few words the method by which you must regulate your senses, take care in all things and under all circumstances, that you be moved and drawn, not by hatred or love of them, but by the will of God alone, loving and hating that only which He wills you to hate or love.

And observe, that I have not given you these methods for regulating the senses that you may dwell upon them; for your mind should almost always be fixed upon the Lord, Who wills that by frequent acts you should apply yourself to conquer your enemies and your sinful passions, both by resisting them, and by making acts of the contrary virtues; but I have taught them to you that you may know how to rule yourself on needful occasions. For you must know, that there is little fruit in a multiplicity of spiritual exercises; which, however excellent in themselves, often lead to mental perplexity, self-love, instability, and the snare of the devil.

XXIV: Of the way to rule the tongue

It is very necessary that the tongue be well bridled and regulated because we are all much inclined to let it run on upon those things which are most pleasing to the senses.

Much speaking springs ordinarily from pride. We persuade ourselves that we know a great deal; we take delight in our own conceits, and endeavor by needless repetitions to impress them on the minds of others, that we may exercise a mastery over them, as though they needed instruction from us.

It is not possible to express in few words the many evils which arise from overmuch speaking.

Talkativeness is the mother of sloth, the sign of ignorance and folly, the door of slander the minister of falsehood, the destroyer of fervent devotion. A multitude of words adds strength to evil passions, by which again the tongue is the more easily led on to indiscreet talking.

Do not indulge in long conversations with those who are unwilling to hear you lest you weary them; nor with those who love to listen to you, lest you exceed the bounds of modesty.

Avoid loud and positive speaking, which is not only odious in itself, but is also a sign of presumption and vanity.

Never speak of thyself or thy doings, nor of thy kindred, except in case of absolute necessity, and then with all possible brevity and reserve. If others seem to speak overmuch of themselves, try to put a favorable construction upon their conduct; but do not imitate it, even though their words seem to tend to self-humiliation and self-accusation.

Speak as little as may be of your neighbor, or of anything concerning him, unless an occasion occurs to say something in his praise.

Speak willingly of God, and especially of His love and goodness; but with fear and caution, lest even here you fall into error: rather take pleasure in listening while others speak of Him, treasuring up their words in the depth of your heart.

Let the sound of men's voices strike only upon your ear; do

you meanwhile lift up your heart to God; and if you must needs listen to their discourse in order to understand and reply to it, yet neglect not to cast your eye in thought to heaven, where God dwelleth, and contemplate His loftiness, as He ever beholds your vileness.

Consider well the things which your heart suggests to you before they pass on to your tongue; for you will perceive that many of them would be better suppressed. Nay, I can still farther assure you, that not a few even of those which you will then think it expedient to speak would be far better buried in silence; and so you will perceive, upon reflection, when the opportunity for speaking is past.

Silence is a strong fortress in the spiritual combat, and a sure pledge of victory.

Silence is the friend of him who distrusts himself and trusts in God; it is the guard of holy prayer, and a wonderful aid in the practice of virtue.

In order to acquire the practice of silence, consider frequently the great benefits which arise therefrom, and the evils and dangers of talkativeness. Love this virtue; and in order to acquire the habit of it, keep silence occasionally, even at times when you might lawfully speak, provided this be not to your own prejudice, or to that of others.

And you will be greatly helped to this by withdrawing from the society of men; for in the place of this, you will have the society of angels, saints, and of God Himself.

Lastly, remember the combat which you have in hand, that, seeing you have so much to do, you may the more willingly refrain from all superfluous words.

XXV: That, in order to fight successfully against his enemies, the Soldier of Christ must avoid as much as possible all perturbation and disquiet of mind

When we have lost our peace of mind, we should do our utmost to recover it; neither is there any accident of life which should reasonably have power to deprive us of that peace, or even to trouble it.

Over our own sins we have indeed cause to mourn deeply; but our sorrow, as I have shown more than once, should be calm; and in like manner, without any disquiet, but with a holy feeling of charity, should we compassionate other sinners, and weep, at least inwardly, over their offenses.

As to other sad and trying events, such as sickness, wounds, or loss of dearest friends, pestilence, re, war, or suchlike evils, though these being painful to nature are for the most part shunned by the men of this world, yet may we, by Divine grace, not only desire, but even love them, as just chastisements upon the wicked, and occasions of virtue to the just. For therefore does our Lord God take pleasure in sending them; and thus borne forward by His will, we shall pass with a calm and quiet spirit through all the bitterness and contradictions of this life. And be assured, that all disquiet on our part is displeasing in His sight; for, of whatever kind it be, it is never free from imperfection, and always springs from some evil root of self-love.

Keep, therefore, a sentinel always on the watch, who, as soon as he shall discern the approach of anything likely to disquiet or disturb you, may give you a signal to take up your weapons of defense.

And consider, that all these evils, and many others of a like kind, though outwardly they appear to be such, are not indeed real evils, nor can they rob us of any real good, but are all ordered or permitted by God for the righteous ends of which we have spoken, or for others most wise and holy, although beyond our power to discern.

So may the most untoward accident work for us much good, if we do but keep our souls in peace and tranquility; otherwise all our exercises will produce little or no fruit.

Besides, when the heart is unquiet it is always exposed to manifold assaults of the enemy: and, moreover, in such a state we are incapable of discerning the right path and the sure way of holiness.

Our enemy, who above all things hates this peace because the Spirit of God dwells and works marvelously therein, often seeks in a friendly disguise to rob us of it, by instilling into our hearts sundry desires which have a semblance of good; but their deceitful nature may be detected by this test among others, that they rob us of our peace of mind

Therefore, to avert so great an evil, when the sentinel gives notice of the approach of some new desire, on no account give it entrance into your heart, until, with a free and unbiased will, you have first presented it to God, and confessing your ignorance and blindness, have earnestly prayed to Him for light to discern whether it comes from Him or from the enemy. Have recourse also, if possible, to the judgment of your spiritual father.

And, even if the desire should be from God, do not begin to carry it into execution till you have mortified your own eagerness; for a work preceded by such mortification will be far more acceptable to Him than if performed with all the impetuosity of nature; nay, sometimes it may be that the mortification will please Him better than the work itself.

Thus, casting from you all evil desires, and not venturing to carry even good desires into effect till you have first repressed your natural impulses, you shall keep the fortress of your heart in security and peace.

And in order to preserve it in perfect peace, you must also guard and defend it from certain inward self-reproaches and remorseful feelings, which are sometimes from the devil, though, as they accuse you of some failing, they seem to come from God. By their fruits shall you know whence they proceed.

If they humble you, if they make you diligent in well-doing, if they take not from you your trust in God, then receive them with all thankfulness as coming from Him. But if they discourage you, if they make you fearful, distrustful, slack and feeble in good deeds, then be assured they come from the enemy; give no ear to them, but continue your exercise.

And as anxiety at the approach of adverse events springs up

even more frequently in our hearts, you have two things to do in order to ward off this assault:

The first is, carefully to search out and discover to what these events are adverse, whether to the soul, or to self-love and self-will.

For, if they be adverse to your own will and to self-love, your chief and greatest enemy, they are not to be called adverse, but to be esteemed special favors and helps from the most high God, to be received with a joyful heart and with thanksgiving.

And though they should be adverse to the soul, you ought not on this account to lose your peace of mind, as I will show you in the following chapter.

The second is, to lift up the heart to God, accepting all things blindly from the hand of His Divine Providence, ever full of manifold blessings beyond your power to comprehend, and seeking to know nothing further.

XXVI: What we should do when we are wounded

When you feel yourself wounded from having weakly, or it may be even willfully and deliberately, fallen into some sin, be not over-fearful or over-anxious, but turn instantly to God, saying:

"Behold, O Lord, what of myself I have done! And what, indeed, could be expected of me but falls?"

And then, after a short pause, humble yourself in your own eyes, mourn over the offense committed against your Lord; and without falling into discouragement, be full of indignation against your evil passions, especially that which has occasioned your fall. Then say:

"Nor even here, Lord, should I have stopped, if Your goodness had not withheld me."

And here give thanks to Him, and love Him more than ever, wondering at the excess of His mercy, Who, when you had so deeply o ended Him, stretched out His right hand to save you from another fall.

Lastly, say, with great confidence in His infinite compassion: "Forgive me, Lord, for Your own sake; suffer me not to depart from You, nor to be separated from You, nor evermore to offend You."

And this done, do not sit down to consider whether God has pardoned you or not; for this is nothing else but pride, restlessness of mind, loss of time, and, under color of various fair pretexts, a delusion of the devil. But, committing yourself unreservedly to the merciful hands of God, pursue your exercise as if you had not fallen.

And if you should fall wounded many times in the day, repeat what I have taught you with no less faith the second, the third, and even the last time than the first; and despising yourself, and hating the sin more and more strive to lead henceforth a life of greater watchfulness.

This exercise is very displeasing to the devil, both because he sees it to be most acceptable to God and also because he is enraged to see himself overcome by one over whom he had been at first victorious. And therefore he seeks by many artful wiles to make us relinquish it; and, through our carelessness and lack of vigilance, he is but too often successful.

The harder therefore, this exercise may seem to you, the greater violence must you do to yourself, renewing it repeatedly even after a single fall.

And if after any fall you feel uneasy, distrustful, and confused in mind, the first thing to be done is to recover your peace and quietness of mind, and with it your confidence in God. Armed with these, turn again to the Lord; for your uneasiness on account of your sin arises not from the consideration of the offense against God, but of the injury to yourself.

To recover this peace, discard entirely from your mind the thought of your fall, and set yourself to meditate on the unspeakable goodness of God; how He is beyond measure ready and willing to forgive every sin, how grievous so-ever; calling the sinner by manifold ways and means to come to Him, that He may unite him to Himself in this life by His grace in order to his sanctification, and in the life to come by His glory for his eternal beatification.

And having quieted your mind by these and the like reflections, turn your thoughts once more to your fall, according to the instructions given you above.

Again, at the time of sacramental confession, to which I exhort you to have recourse frequently, call to mind all your falls, and with renewed sorrow and indignation at the offense against God, and renewed purpose never again to o end Him, disclose them with all sincerity to your spiritual father.

The Enemy's Deceptions

XXVII: Of the means employed by the Devil to assail and deceive those who desire to give themselves up to the practice of virtue, and those who are already entangled in the bondage of sin

You must know, that the devil is intent upon nothing but our ruin, and that he does not use the same method of assault with all persons.

In order, then, to make known to you some of his modes of attack, his stratagems and devices, I will set before you several different conditions of men.

- ❖ Some remain in the service of sin without a thought of escape.
- ❖ Some would fain be free, but never make the attempt.
- ❖ Others think they are walking in the way of holiness, while they are wandering far from it.
- ❖ And lastly, some, after having attained unto holiness, fall into deeper perdition.

We will discourse separately of each.

XXVIII: Of the Devil's assaults and devices against those whom he holds in the bondage of sin

When the devil holds a man in the bondage of sin, his chief

care is to blind his eyes more and more, and to avert from him everything which might lead to a knowledge of his most wretched condition.

And not only does he, by instilling contrary thoughts, drive from him all reflections and inspirations which call him to conversion, but, by affording him ready opportunities, he makes him fall into other and greater sins. Hence, the thicker and darker waxes his blindness, the more desperate and habitual becomes his course of sin; and thus, from blindness to deeper blindness, from sin to fouler sin, his wretched life will whirl on even unto death, unless God, by His grace, should intervene to save him. The remedy for one in this unhappy condition is, to be ready to give diligent heed to the thoughts and inspirations which call him from darkness to light, crying with all his heart to his Creator, "O Lord, help me; help me speedily; leave me not any longer in the darkness of sin." And let him not fail to repeat this cry for mercy over and over again in these or the like words.

If possible, let him have immediate recourse to some spiritual guide, and ask aid and counsel, that so he may be delivered from the power of the enemy.

And if he cannot do this at the moment, let him fly with all speed to the crucifix, prostrating himself before it; and asking mercy and aid also from the Mother of God.

On this speed does the victory depend, as you will learn in the next chapter.

XXIX: Of the arts and stratagems by which he holds in bondage those who knowing their misery, would fain be free; and how it is that our resolutions prove so often ineffectual

When a man begins to perceive the evil of his life, and to desire to change it, the devil often deludes and overcomes him by such means as these:

"Presently, presently."

"Cras, cras" (tomorrow, tomorrow) as the raven cries.

"I wish first to consider and dispatch this business, this perplexity, that I may then be able to give myself with greater tranquility to spiritual things."

This is a snare in which many men have been, and are still daily, entangled; and the cause of this is our own negligence and heedlessness, seeing that, in a matter touching the honor of God and the salvation of the soul, we neglect to seize instantly that effectual weapon: "Now, now;" wherefore "presently?" "Today, today;" wherefore "tomorrow?" saying each one to himself:

"Even supposing this 'presently' and this 'tomorrow' should be granted to me, is it the way of safety and of victory to seek first to be wounded and to commit fresh disorders?"

You see, then, that the way to escape this snare, and that mentioned in the preceding chapter, and to subdue the enemy, is, to yield prompt obedience to all heavenly thoughts and inspirations.

Prompt obedience, I say, and not mere resolutions; for these are often fallacious, and many have been deceived thereby from various causes.

First. Because our resolutions are not founded upon self-distrust and trust in God. But our excessive pride, whence proceeds this blindness and delusion, prevents our perceiving it.

The light to see and the medicine to cure it both proceed from the goodness of God Who suffers us to fall that He may recall us thereby from self-confidence to confidence in Him alone, and from pride to self-knowledge.

Your resolutions, therefore, to be effectual, must be steadfast; and to be steadfast, they must be free from all self-confidence, and humbly based on confidence in God.

Second. When we are making our resolutions, we dwell on the beauty and excellence of virtue, which attracts our will, slack and feeble as it is; but when confronted by the difficulties which attend the attainment of virtue, the weak and untried will fail and draw back.

Learn, therefore, to love the difficulties which attend the attainment of all virtues more than even the virtues themselves, and use these difficulties in various measures to strengthen your will, if you desire in good earnest to acquire these virtues.

And know, that the more courageously and lovingly you shall embrace these difficulties, the more speedy and complete shall be your victory over self and all your other enemies.

Third. In our resolutions we too often look rather to our own advantage than to the will of God and the acquisition of the virtues He requires of us. This is frequently the case with resolutions made in times of great spiritual joy or acute sorrow, when we seem unable to find any relief but in a resolution to give ourselves wholly to God and to the practice of virtue.

To avoid this snare, take care in times of spiritual consolation to be very cautious and humble in your resolutions, especially in your vows and promises; and in tribulation let your resolution be to bear your cross patiently, according to the will of God, nay, to exalt it, refusing all earthly, and if so be even all heavenly consolation. Let your one desire, your one prayer, be that God would help you to bear all adverse things, keeping the virtue of patience unstained, and giving no displeasure to your Lord.

XXX: Of a delusion of those who imagine they are going onward to perfection

Our malignant foe, thus repulsed in his first and second assault and stratagem, has recourse to a third, which is, to turn away our attention from the enemies who are close at hand to injure and assail us, and to fill us with resolutions and desires after higher degrees of perfection.

Hence we are continually being wounded; yet we pay no attention to our wounds, and looking upon these resolutions as already fulfilled, we take pride in them in various ways.

And while we cannot endure the least thing or the slightest word which crosses our will, we were our time in long meditations and resolutions to endure the acutest sufferings on earth or in purgatory for the love of God.

And because our inferior part feels no repugnance at these things in the distance, we flatter ourselves, miserable creatures as we are, into the conceit that we belong to the class of patient and heroic sufferers.

To avoid this snare, resolve to fight manfully against the enemies who are close at hand, and actually waging war against you. You will thus discover whether your resolutions are real or imaginary, weak or strong; and so you will go on to virtue and perfection by the beaten and royal road.

But against enemies who are not wont to trouble you I do not advise you to take up arms, unless there appear a probability of their making an attack at some future time. In this case it is lawful to make resolutions beforehand, that you may be found strong and prepared.

Do not, however, judge of your resolutions by their effects, even though you should have long and faithfully exercised your- self in virtue; but be very humble with regard to them; fear yourself and your own weakness, and trust in God, and seek His help by frequent prayer to strengthen and preserve you in all dangers, and especially from the very slightest presumption or self-confidence.

For in this case, though we may not be able to overcome some slight defects which our Lord sometimes leaves in us in order to greater, humility and self-knowledge, and for the protection of some virtue, we may yet be permitted to form purposes of aspiring to higher degrees of perfection.

XXXI: Of the Devil's assaults and stratagems in order to draw us away from the path of holiness

The fourth device of the Evil One, when he sees us advancing steadily towards holiness, is, to excite within us a variety of good desires, that by this means he may lead us away from the exercise of virtue into sin.

A sick person is perhaps bearing his illness with a patient

will. The cunning adversary knows that by this means he may attain to a habit of patience; and he immediately sets before him all the good works which in a different condition he might be able to perform, and tries to persuade him that if he were but well he would be able to serve God better, and be more useful to himself and others.

Having once aroused such wishes within him, he goes on increasing them by degrees, till he makes him restless at the impossibility of carrying them into effect; and the deeper and stronger such wishes become, the more does this restlessness increase. Then the enemy leads him on gently, and with a stealthy step, to impatience at the sickness, not as sickness, but as a hindrance to those good works which he so anxiously desires to perform for some greater good.

When he has brought him thus far, with the same art he removes from his mind the end he had in view, to serve God and perform good works, and leaves him only the bare desire to be rid of his sickness. And then, if this does not happen according to his wish, he is so much troubled as to become actually impatient; and so unconsciously he falls from the virtue in which he was exercising himself into the opposite vice.

The way to guard against and resist this snare is, to be very careful, when in a state of trial, not to give way to desires after any good work, which, being out of your power to execute, would very probably disquiet you.

In such cases, resign yourself with all patience, resignation, and humility to the conviction that your desires would not have the effect you think, inasmuch as you are far more insignificant and unstable than you account yourself to be.

Or else believe that God, in His surer counsels, or on account of your unworthiness, is not pleased to accept this work at your hand, but will rather that you should patiently abase and humble yourself under the gentle and mighty hand of His will.

In like manner, if prevented by your spiritual father, or in any other way, from attending as frequently as you desire to your devotions, and especially Holy Communion, suffer not yourself to be troubled or disquieted by longings after them, but, casting off all that is your own, clothe yourself with the good pleasure of your Lord, saying within yourself:

"If the eye of Divine Providence had not perceived sin and ingratitude in me, I should not now be deprived of the blessing of receiving the most holy Sacrament; but since my Lord thus makes known to me my unworthiness, be His holy name for ever blessed and praised. I trust, O Lord, that in Your infinite loving-kindness You will so rule my heart, that it may please You in all things in doing or suffering Your will; that it may open before You, so that, entering into it spiritually, You may comfort and strengthen it against the enemies who seek to draw it away from You. Thus may all be done as seems good in Your sight. My Creator and Redeemer, may Your will be now and ever my food and sustenance! This one favor only do I beg of You, O my Beloved, that my soul, freed and purified from everything displeasing to You, and adorned with all virtues, may be ever prepared for Your coming, and for whatsoever it may please You to do with me."

If you will observe these rules, know for certain that, when baffled in any good work which you have a desire to perform, be the hindrance from the devil, to disquiet you and turn you aside from the way of virtue, or be it from God, to make trial of your submission to His will, you will still have an opportunity of pleasing your Lord in the way most acceptable to Him. And herein consists true devotion, and the service which God requires of us.

I warn you, also, lest you grow impatient under trials, from whatever source proceeding, that in using the lawful means which God's servants are wont to use, you use them not with the desire and hope to obtain relief, but because it is the will of God that they should be used; for we know not whether His Divine Majesty will be pleased by their means to deliver us.

Otherwise you will fall into further evils; for if the event should not fulfill your purpose and desires, you will easily fall into impatience, or your patience will be defective, not wholly acceptable to God, and of little value.

Lastly, I would here warn you of a hidden deceit of our self-love, which is wont on certain occasions to cover and justify our faults. For instance, a sick man who has but little patience under his sickness conceals his impatience under the cover of zeal for some apparent good; saying, that his vexation arises not really from impatience under his sufferings, but is a reasonable sorrow, because he has incurred it by his own fault, or else because others are harassed or wearied by the trouble he gives them, or by some other cause.

In like manner, the ambitious man, who frets after some unattained honor, does not attribute his discontent to his own pride and vanity, but to some other cause, which he knows full well would give him no concern did it not touch himself. So neither would the sick man care if they, whose fatigue and trouble on his account seems to give him so much vexation, should have the same care and trouble on account of the sickness of another. A plain proof that the root of such men's sorrow is not concern for others, or anything else, but an abhorrence of everything that crosses their own will.

Therefore, to avoid this and other errors, bear patiently, as I have told you, every trial and every sorrow, from whatever cause arising.

XXXII: Of the above named last assault and stratagem by which the Devil seeks to make the virtues we have acquired the occasions of our ruin

The cunning and malicious serpent fails not to tempt us by his artifices even by means of the very virtues we have acquired, that, leading us to regard them and ourselves with complacency, they may become our ruin; exalting us on high, that we may fall into the sin of pride and vainglory.

To preserve yourself from this danger, choose for your battlefield the safe and level ground of a true and deep conviction of your own nothingness, that you are nothing, that you know nothing, that you can do nothing, and have nothing but misery and sin, and deserve nothing but eternal damnation.

Entrench yourself firmly within the limits of this truth, and suffer not yourself to be enticed so much as a hair's breadth therefrom by any evil thought, or anything else that may befall you; knowing well that there are so many enemies, who would slay or wound you should you fall into their hands.

In order to acquit yourself well in this exercise of the true knowledge of your own nothingness, observe the following rule:

> As often as you reflect upon yourself and your own works, consider always what you are of yourself, and not what you are by the aid of God's grace, and so esteem yourself as you shall thus find yourself to be.

Consider first the time before you were in existence, and you will see yourself to have been during all that abyss of eternity a mere nothing, and that you did nothing, and could have done nothing, towards giving yourself an existence.

Next consider the time since you did receive a being from the sole bounty of God. And here, also, if you leave to Him that which is His own (His continual care of you, which sustains you every moment of your life), what are you of yourself but still a mere nothing?

For, undoubtedly, were He to leave you for one moment to yourself, you would instantly return to that first nothingness from whence you were drawn by His Almighty Hand.

It is plain that, in the order of nature, and viewed in yourself alone, you have no reason to esteem yourself, or to desire the esteem of others.

Again, in the life of grace and the performance of good works, what good or meritorious deed could your nature perform by itself if deprived of Divine assistance? For, considering, on the other hand, the multitude of your past transgressions, and more- over the multitude of other sins from which God's compassionate Hand has alone withheld you, you will find that your iniquities, being multiplied not only by days and years, but by acts and habits of sin (one evil habit drawing another after it), would have swelled to an almost infinite amount, and so have made of you another infernal Lucifer. Hence, if you would not rob God of the praise of His goodness, but cleave faithfully to Him, you must learn day-by-day to think more humbly of yourself.

And be very careful to deal justly in this judgment of yourself, or it may do you no little injury.

For if in the knowledge of your own iniquity you surpass a man who, in his blindness, accounts himself to be something, you will lose exceedingly, and fall far below him in the action of the will, if you desire to be esteemed and regarded by men for that which you know yourself not to be.

If, then, you desire that the consciousness of your vileness and sinfulness should protect you from your enemies, and make you dear to God, you must not only despise yourself, as unworthy of any good and deserving of every evil, but you must love to be despised by others, detesting honors, rejoicing in shame, and stooping on all occasions to offices which others hold in contempt. You must make no account at all of their judgment, lest you be thereby deterred from this holy exercise. But take care that the end in view be solely your own humiliation and self-discipline, lest you be in any degree influenced by a certain lurking pride and spirit of presumption, which, under some specious pretext or other, often causes us to make little or no account of the opinions of others.

And should you perchance come to be loved, esteemed, or praised by others for any good gift bestowed on you by God, be not moved a single step thereby; but collect yourself steadily within the stronghold of this true and just judgment of yourself, first turning to God and saying to Him with all your heart:

"O Lord, never let me rob You of Your honor and the glory of Your grace; to You be praise and honor and glory, to me confusion of face." And then say mentally of him who praises you: "Whence is it that he accounts me good, since truly my God and His works are alone good?"

For by thus giving back to the Lord that which is His own, you will keep your enemies afar off, and prepare yourself to receive greater gifts and favors from your God.

And if the remembrance of good works expose you to any risk of vanity, view them instantly, not as your own, but as God's; and say to them: "I know not how you did appear and originate in my mind, for you derived not your being from me; but the good God and His grace created, nourished, and preserved you. Him alone, then, will I acknowledge as your true and first Parent, Him will I thank, and to Him will I return all the praise."

Consider next, that not only do all the works which you have done fall short of the light which has been given you to know them, and the grace to execute them, but also that in them- selves they are very imperfect, and fall very short of that pure intention and due diligence and fervor with which they should be performed, and which should always accompany them.

If, then, you will well consider this, you will see reason rather for shame than for vain complacency, because it is but too true that the graces which we receive pure and perfect from God are sullied in their use by our imperfections.

Again, compare your works with those of the saints and other servants of God; for by such comparison you will find that your best and greatest are of base alloy, and of little worth.

Next, measure them by those which Christ wrought for you in the mystery of His life, and of His continual Cross; and setting aside the consideration of His Divinity, view His works in them- selves alone; consider both the fervor and the purity of the love with which they were wrought, and you will see that all your works are indeed as nothing.

And lastly, if you will raise your thoughts to the Divinity and the boundless Majesty of your God, and the service which He deserves at your hands, you will see plainly that your works should excite in you not vanity but fear.

Therefore, in all your ways, in all your works, however holy they may be, you must cry unto your Lord with all your heart, saying: "God be merciful to me a sinner."

Further, I would advise you to be very reserved in making known the gifts which God may have bestowed on you; for this is almost always displeasing to your Lord, as He Himself plainly shows us in the following lesson.

Appearing once in the form of a child to a devout servant of His, she asked Him, with great simplicity, to recite the angelical salutation. He readily began: "*Ave Maria, gratia plena, Dominus tecum, benedicta tu in mulieribus,*" and then stopped, being unwilling to praise Himself in the words which follow. And while she was praying Him to proceed, He withdrew Himself from her, leaving His servant full of consolation because of the heavenly doctrine which, by His example, He had thus revealed to her.

Do you also learn to humble yourself, and to acknowledge yourself, with all your works, to be the nothing which you are.

This is the foundation of all other virtues. God, before we existed, created us out of nothing; and now that we exist through Him, He wills that the whole spiritual edifice should be built on this foundation the knowledge that of ourselves we are nothing. And the deeper we dig into this knowledge, the higher will the building rise. And in proportion as we clear away the earth of our own misery, the Divine Architect will bring solid stones for its completion.

And never imagine that you can dig deep enough; on the contrary, think this of yourself, that if anything belonging to a creature could be infinite, it would be your unworthiness.

With this knowledge, duly carried into practice, we possess all good; without it we are little better than nothing, though we should do the works of all the saints, and be continually absorbed in God.

O blessed knowledge, which makes us happy on earth, and blessed in heaven! O light, which, issuing from darkness, makes the soul bright and clear! O unknown joy, which sparkles amid our impurities! O nothingness, which, once known, makes us lords of all!

I should never weary of telling you this: if you would give praise to God, accuse yourself, and desire to be accused by others. Humble yourself with all, and below all, if you would exalt Him in yourself and yourself in Him.

Would you find Him? Exalt not yourself, or He will fly from you. Abase yourself to the utmost, and He will seek you and embrace you.

And the more you humble yourself in your own sight, and the more you delight to be accounted vile by others, and to be spurned as a thing abominable, the more lovingly will He esteem and embrace you. Account yourself unworthy of so great a grace bestowed on you by your God, Who suffered shame for you in order to unite you to Himself. Fail not to return Him continual thanks; and be grateful to those who have been the occasion of your humiliation, and still more to those who have trampled you under their feet, thinking that you have endured it reluctantly, and not with your own goodwill. Yet were it even so, you must suffer no outward token of reluctance to escape you.

If, notwithstanding all these considerations, which are only too true, the cunning of the devil and our own ignorance and evil inclinations should yet prevail over us, so that thoughts of self-exaltation will still molest us and make an impression on our hearts, then is the time to humble ourselves the more profoundly in our own sight; for we see by this proof that we have advanced but a little way in the spiritual life and in true self-knowledge, inasmuch as we are unable to free ourselves from those annoyances which spring from the root of our empty pride. So shall we extract honey from the poison and healing from the wound.

Virtues

XXXIII: Some counsels as to the overcoming of evil passions and the acquisition of virtue

Though I have said so much on the course to be pursued in order to conquer self and adorn it with all virtues, there still remain some other points concerning which I would give you some advice.

1. In your endeavors after holiness, never, be persuaded to use such spiritual exercises as select formally different virtues for different days of the week, setting apart one for the attainment of each. But let the order of your warfare and your exercise be to combat those passions which have always injured and still continue to assault and injure you; and to adorn yourself, and that with all possible perfection, with their contrary virtues.

For having once acquired these virtues, all others will be readily attained, as occasion offers, with little comparative exertion. And occasions will never be wanting; for all the virtues are linked together in one chain, and he who possesses one in perfection has all the others ready on the threshold of his heart.

2. Never set a fixed time, such as days, or weeks, or years, for the attainment of any virtue; but, as an infant newly born, a soldier just enlisted, fight your way continually towards the summit of perfection. Never stand still, even for a moment; for to stand still in the way of virtue and perfection is not to regain breath or courage, but to fall back, or to grow feebler

than before.

By standing still, I mean flattering ourselves that we have perfectly acquired the virtue in question, and so taking less heed of the occasions which call us to fresh acts of it, or of little failures therein.

Therefore be careful, be fervent, be watchful, that you neglect not the slightest opportunity of exercising any virtue. Love all such occasions, and especially those which are attended with the greatest difficulty, because habits are quickest formed and deepest rooted when the difficulties to be overcome are greatest; love those occasions, therefore, which present such difficulties.

Fly those only, and that with rapid step, with all diligence and speed, which might lead to the temptation of the flesh.

3.   Be prudent and discreet in those exercises which may prove injurious to bodily health, such as self-chastisement by means of disciplines, hair-cloths, fasts, vigils, meditations, and the like; for these virtues must be acquired slowly and by degrees, as will be hereafter explained.

As to other virtues which are wholly internal, such as the love of God, contempt of the world, self-abasement, hatred of vicious passions and of sin, meekness and patience, love towards all men, towards those who injure us and the like, it is not necessary to acquire these gradually, nor to mount by degrees to perfection therein; but you should strive at once with all your might to practice each with all possible perfection.

4.   Let your whole heart desire nothing, think of nothing, crave nothing, long for nothing, but to conquer that passion with which you are struggling, and to attain its contrary virtue. Be this your world, your heaven, your earth, your whole treasure; and all with the sole view to please God. Whether eating or fasting, laboring or resting, watching or sleeping, at home or abroad, whether engaged in devotion or in manual labor, let all be directed to the conquest and extinction of this passion, and to the attainment of the contrary virtue.

5.   Wage unceasing war against earthly pleasures and comforts, so will no vice have much power to assail you. For all

vices spring from this one root of pleasure; when this, therefore, is cut away by hatred of self, they lose their strength and power.

For if with one hand you will try to fight against some particular sin or pleasure, and with the other dally with other earthly enjoyments, though their guilt be not mortal, but only venial, your battles will be hard and bloody, your victories infrequent and uncertain. Keep, therefore, constantly in mind these divine words: "He that loveth his life shall lose it, and he that hateth his life in this world keepeth it unto life eternal." John 12:25. "Brethren, we are debtors not to the flesh, to live according to the flesh. For if you live according to the flesh, you shall die."

6.   Lastly, it would be well, it may be even necessary, for you to make in the first place a general confession, with all the necessary conditions, that you may be the better assured of your Lord's favor, to whom alone you must look for all grace and victory.

XXXIV: Virtues are to be gradually acquired by exercising ourselves in their various degrees, and giving our attention first to one and then to another

Although the true servant of Christ who aspires to perfection should set no limit to his advancement, there are some kinds of spiritual fervor which require to be restrained with a certain discretion, lest, being embraced too ardently at first, they should give way and leave us in the midst of our course. Hence, besides what has been said as to moderation in exterior exercises, we have to learn, moreover, that even interior virtues are best acquired gradually, and in their due order; for thus what is small in the beginning soon becomes great and permanent. Thus, for instance, we should not ordinarily attempt to rejoice in afflictions, and to desire them, till we have first passed through the lower degrees of the virtue of patience.

Neither would I have you give your chief attention to all or to many virtues at once, but first to one and then to the others; for thus will the virtuous habit be more easily and firmly planted in the soul. For by the constant exercise of a single virtue the memory recurs to it more promptly on all occasions, the intellect grows quicker to discern new methods and reasons for attaining it, and the will inclines more readily and fervently to its pursuit, than if occupied with many virtues at one and the same time.

And, by means of the uniformity of the exercise, the acts which relate to any single virtue are produced with less e ort from the conformity between them. The one calls forth and aids his fellow; and by their mutual resemblance they make a deeper impression upon the heart, which is prepared and disposed for the reception of new seed by having already brought forth similar fruits.

These reasons have the greater force, as we know assuredly that whoever exercises himself well in one virtue learns at the same time how to exercise himself in another; and thus, by the inseparable connection between them, all grow together with the increase of one, as rays proceeding from one and the same Divine light.

XXXV: Of the means whereby virtues are ac- quired, and how we should use then so as to attend for some considerable time to one virtue only

For the attainment of holiness we need, besides all that has been already described, a great and generous heart, a will that is neither slack nor remiss, but firm and resolute, and withal a certain expectation of having to pass through many bitter and adverse trials.

And further, there are particular inclinations and affections which we may acquire by frequently considering how pleasing they are to God, how excellent and noble in themselves, and how useful and necessary to us, inasmuch as from them and in them all perfection has its origin and end.

Let us, then, make a steadfast resolution every morning to exercise ourselves therein according to the occasions which may arise in the course of the day; during which we should often ex- amine ourselves, to see whether or not we have fulfilled them, renewing them afterwards more earnestly, and all this with especial reference to that virtue which we have in hand.

So also, let the examples of the saints, and our prayers and meditations on the life and passion of Christ, which are so needful in every spiritual exercise, be applied principally to the particular virtue in which we are for the time exercising ourselves.

Let us do the same on all occasions which may arise, however various in kind, as we shall presently explain more particularly. Let us so inure ourselves to acts of virtue, both interior and exterior, that we may come at last to perform them with the same promptness and facility with which in times past we performed others agreeable to our natural will. And, as we said before, the more opposed such acts are to these natural wishes, the more speedily will the good habit be introduced into our soul.

The sacred words of Holy Scripture, either uttered with the lips or pondered in the heart, as may best suit our case, have a marvelous power to aid us in this exercise. We should therefore have many such in readiness to bear upon the virtue we wish to practice; and these we should repeat continually throughout the day, and especially at each rising of the rebellious passion. For instance, if we are striving to attain the virtue of patience, we may repeat the following words, or others like them:

- ❖ "My children, suffer patiently the wrath which is come upon you" (Baruch 4:25)
- ❖ "The patience of the poor shall not perish forever" (Psalm 9:18)
- ❖ "The patient man is better than the valiant; and he that ruleth his spirit, than he that taketh cities" (Proverbs

16:32)

- ❖ "In your patience you shall possess your souls" (Luke 21:19)
- ❖ "Let us run by patience to the fight proposed to us" (Hebrews12:1)

To the same end we may, in like manner, use such prayers as the following:

- ❖ "When, O my God, shall this heart of mine be armed with the buckler of patience?"
- ❖ "When shall I learn to bear every trouble with a quiet mind, that so I may please my Lord?"
- ❖ "O most dear sufferings, which liken me unto my Lord Jesus, crucified for me!"
- ❖ "Only life of my soul I shall ever, for Your glory, live contented amid a thousand torments!"
- ❖ "How blessed shall I be, if, in the midst of the re of tribulation, I burn with the desire of even greater sufferings!"
- ❖ Let us use these short prayers, and others suitable to our advancement in holiness, that we may acquire the spirit of devotion.

These short prayers are called ejaculations, because they are darted like javelins towards heaven. They have great power to excite us to virtue; and will penetrate even to the heart of God, if only they have these two accompaniments for their wings:

- ❖ The one a full certainty that our exercise of virtue is well-pleasing to our God.
- ❖ The other, a true and fervent desire for the attainment of virtue, for the sole end of pleasing His Divine Majesty.

XXXVI: That in the exercise of virtue we must proceed with unceasing watchfulness

One of the most important and necessary means for the attainment of virtue, besides what has been already taught, is to press forward continually to the end we have proposed to ourselves, lest by standing still we fall back.

For when we cease to produce acts of virtue, many unruly passions are generated within us by the violent inclination of the sensitive appetite, and by other exterior influences, whereby virtue is destroyed, or at least diminished; and moreover, we thus lose many gifts and graces with which our Lord might have rewarded our further progress. Therefore is the spiritual journey different from the course of the earthly traveler; for he, by standing still, loses nothing of the ground already gained as is the case with him who travels heavenward.

And moreover, the weariness of the earthly pilgrim increases with the continuance of his bodily motion; while, in the spiritual journey, the farther a man advances, the more does his vigor and strength increase.

For, by the exercise of virtue, the resistance of the inferior part of the soul, which made the way hard and wearisome, grows daily weaker; while the superior part, wherein the virtue resides, is in the same proportion established and strengthened.

Hence, as we advance in holiness, the pain which accompanied the progress gradually diminishes; and a certain secret joy, which, by the Divine operation, is mingled with that pain, increases hourly more and more. And thus, proceeding with increasing ease and delight from virtue to virtue, we reach at last the mountaintop; where the perfected spirit henceforth labors without weariness but, rather with joy and ecstasy because, having now tamed and conquered its unruly passions, and overcome itself and all created things, it dwells forever blessed in the bosom of the Most High, and there, while sweetly laboring, takes its rest.

XXXVII: That, as we must always continue in the exercise of all the virtues, so we must not shun any opportunity which offers for their attainment

We have seen very clearly that we must go forward without ever stopping in the way of perfection.

To this end, we ought to be very careful and vigilant not to let slip any opportunity which may present itself for the attainment of any virtue. For they have very little knowledge of this way who avoid as much as they can all such adverse things as might greatly assist their progress.

For, not to forget my accustomed advice, if you would acquire the habit of patience, it is not expedient to avoid those persons, actions, or thoughts which move you to impatience.

Withdraw not, therefore, from the society of any one because it is disagreeable; but whilst conversing and holding intercourse with those who most annoy you keep your will always ready and disposed to endure whatever may befall you, however wearisome and annoying; for otherwise you will never learn to be patient.

In like manner, if you find any occupation irksome, either in itself, or because of the person who imposed it on you, or because it hinders you from doing something else more pleasing, do not therefore shrink from undertaking and persevering in it, though it disquiet you, and though you think to find peace by neglecting it; for this would be no true peace, as proceeding not from a soul purified from passion and adorned with virtues, neither could you ever in this way learn to suffer.

I would say the same of harassing thoughts, which at times will annoy and disturb your mind. There is no need to drive them entirely from you; for besides the pain they occasion, they accustom you also to bear contradiction.

And to give you contrary advice, would be to teach you rather to shun labor than to attain to that virtue which you have in view.

It is very true that it becomes every man, and especially the tried soldier, to defend himself on these occasions with vigilance and dexterity; now confronting his enemies, now evading them, according to the measure of spiritual strength and virtue which he has attained.

But, for all this, he must never actually turn back and retreat, so as to leave behind all opposition; for even if we thereby save ourselves for the time from the peril of falling, we shall risk exposing ourselves more to future attacks of temptation, not being armed and fortified beforehand by the exercise of the contrary virtue.

This counsel, however, applies not to the sins of the flesh, of which we have already spoken more particularly.

XXXVIII: That we should highly esteem all opportunities of fighting for the acquisition of virtues, and chiefly of those which present the greatest difficulties

I shall not be contented to have you simply not shun the opportunities which may present themselves of attaining the different virtues; I would have you esteem them as things of great price and value, seek and embrace them joyfully whenever they present themselves, and account those dearest and most precious which are most repugnant to nature.

To this, by the Divine assistance, you will be enabled to attain by impressing strongly upon your mind the following considerations:

First, that opportunities are means adapted, nay, necessary, for the attainment of virtue. When, therefore, you pray to the Lord for any virtue, you at the same time ask for occasions to exercise it; else would your prayer be vain, and you would be contradicting yourself and tempting your God, Who does not usually give patience without tribulation, nor humility without humiliations.

The same may be said of all virtues, which are most surely attained by means of Crosses. And the more painful these are, the more effectually do they aid us, and therefore the more acceptable and welcome should they be. For acts of virtue performed in such circumstances are more generous and energetic, and open to us an easier and more speedy way to virtue.

But we ought also to value, and not to leave without its appropriate exercise, the most trifling occasion, though it be but a word or a look, which crosses our will; because the acts thus produced are more frequent, though less intense, than those called forth by circumstances of great difficulty.

The other consideration (of which we have already spoken) is, that all events which befall us come from God for our good, in order that we may derive fruit therefrom.

And although, as we have said before, some of these occasions, such as our own defects, or those of others, cannot be said to be of God, Who wills not sin, yet are they from Him, inasmuch as He permits them, and though able to hinder them, hinders them not. But all the sorrows and afflictions which come upon us, either by our own fault or the malice of others, are both from God and of God, because He concurs in them; and that which He would not have us do, as being full of a deformity beyond measure hateful to His most pure eyes, He would yet have us suffer, for our greater advancement in holiness, or for some other wise reason unknown to us.

Seeing, then, that it is most assuredly our Lord's will that we should suffer willingly any Cross which may come upon us, either from others or from our own evil deeds, to say, as many do in excuse for their impatience, that God wills not evil, but abhors it, is a vain pretext, whereby to cover our own faults, and avoid the Cross which He wills us to bear.

Nay, I will say further, that supposing all other circumstances the same, our Lord is more pleased with our patient endurance of trials which come upon us from the wickedness of men, especially of those whom we have served and benefited, than with our endurance of other grievous annoyances. And this because our proud nature is, for the most part, more humbled by the former than by the latter; and also because by willingly enduring them we do above measure please and magnify our God, cooperating with Him in that wherein His fine able goodness and omnipotence shine forth most brightly, namely, in extracting from the deadly poison of malice and wickedness the sweet and precious fruit of holiness and virtue.

No sooner, therefore, does our Lord perceive in us an earnest desire to attempt and persevere in so glorious an undertaking than He prepares for us a chalice of strongest temptation and hardest trial, that we may drink it at the appointed hour; and we, recognizing therein His love and our own good, should receive it willingly and blindly, confidently and promptly drinking it to the very dregs, as a medicine compounded by a Hand which cannot err of ingredients the more pro table to the soul in proportion to their intrinsic bitterness.

XXXIX: How to avail ourselves of various occasions for the exercise of a single virtue

We have already seen that it is more pro table to exercise our- selves for a time in a single virtue than in many at once; and that we should use with this view the occasions we meet with, how- ever various. Now learn how to accomplish this with tolerable facility.

It may happen that in the same day, or even in the same hour, we are reproved for something in which we have done well, or blamed on some other account; we may be harshly refused some favor we have asked, it may be a mere tri e; we may be unjustly suspected; or we may be called upon to endure some bodily pain, or some petty annoyance, such as a dish badly cooked; or some more heavy affliction and harder to be borne, such as this wretched life is full of, may befall us.

Though, in the variety of these or similar occurrences, we may perform various acts of virtue, yet, if we would keep to the rule laid down, we shall continue to exercise ourselves in acts wholly conformable to the virtue we have at the time in hand; as, for example:

❖ If, when these occasions present themselves, we are

exercising ourselves in patience, we shall endure them
all willingly and with a joyful heart.

❖ If our exercise be of humility, we shall in all these little
crosses acknowledge ourselves to be deserving of every
possible ill.

❖ If of obedience, we shall submit ourselves at once to
the almighty hand of God, as well as to all created
things, whether rational or even inanimate, which may
have caused us these annoyances, and this to please
Him, because He has so willed it.

❖ If of poverty, we shall be well content to be stripped
and robbed of all earthly consolations, whether great or
small.

❖ If of charity, we shall produce acts of love towards our
neighbor as the instrument of good to us, and towards
our Lord God as the first and loving cause whence these annoyances proceed, or by whom they are permitted
for our spiritual exercise and improvement.

From what has been said of the various accidents which
may befall us daily, we may also learn how, during a single trial
of long duration, such as sickness or other like affliction, we
may yet continue to produce acts of that virtue in which we are
at the time exercising ourselves.

XL: Of the time to be given to the exercise of each virtue, and of the signs of our progress

It is not for me to determine the time to be given to the exercise of each several virtue. This must be regulated by the
state and necessities of individuals, by the progress they are
making in their spiritual course, and by the judgment of their
director.

But if we set ourselves faithfully and diligently to work after
the manner I have described, there is no doubt but that in a
few weeks' time we shall have made no little progress.

It is a sign of advancement in holiness if we persevere in our exercises of virtue amid dryness, darkness, and anguish of spirit, and the withdrawal of spiritual consolation.

Another clear indication will be the degree of resistance made by the senses to the performance of acts of virtue; for the weaker this resistance, the greater will be our progress. When, therefore, we cease to experience any opposition or rebellion in the inferior and sensual part, and more especially in sudden and unexpected assaults, we may look upon it as a sign that we have acquired the virtue.

The greater the alacrity and joyfulness of spirit which accompanies these acts, the greater may be our hope that we have derived pro t from this exercise. We must beware, however, of assuming as a certainty that we have acquired any virtue, or entirely subdued any one passion, even though after a long time, and after many struggles, we may have ceased to feel its motions within us. For here also the arts and devices of Satan and our own deceitful nature may find place, since that which is really vice seems to our lurking pride to be virtue. Besides, if we look to the perfection to which God calls us, we shall hardly persuade ourselves, however great the progress we have made in the way of holiness, that we have even crossed its threshold.

Return, therefore, to your first exercises, as a young soldier, and a newborn babe, but just beginning to struggle, as if you had hitherto done nothing.

And remember to attend rather to advancement in holiness than to an examination of your progress; for the Lord God, the true and only Searcher of our hearts, gives this knowledge to some and withholds it from others, according as He sees that it will lead to pride or to humility; and as a loving Father He removes a danger from one, while to another He offers an opportunity of increase in holiness. Therefore, although the soul perceive not her progress, let her continue these her exercises; for she shall see it when it shall please the Lord, for her greater good, to make it known to her.

XLI: That we must not yield to the wish to be delivered from the trials we are patiently enduring, and how we are to regulate all our desires so as to advance in holiness

When you shall find yourself in any painful position, and bear it patiently, take heed lest the devil or your own self-love persuade you to desire deliverance from it; for you may thereby incur two great evils:

- ❖ First. If this desire should not rob you at once of the virtue of patience, it would at least gradually dispose you to impatience.
- ❖ Second. Your patience would become defective, and would be rewarded by God only according to the duration of the suffering; whereas if you had not desired to be freed from it, but had committed yourself wholly to His Divine goodness, your sufferings, though but of an hour's duration, or even less, would have been accepted by your Lord as an enduring service.

In this, then, and in all things, make it your unvarying rule to keep your wishes so far removed from every other object that they may tend simply to their true and only end, the Will of God. For thus will they be ever right and true; and in any cross-accident which may occur, you will be not only tranquil but content, because, as nothing can happen without the Supreme Will, by willing the same you will come at all times both to will all that happens and to possess all that you desire.

This must not be understood either of our own sins or those of others, for God wills not these; but it applies to every chastisement arising from them or from any other cause, though it be so keen and searching as to reach the very bottom of the heart, and to wither the very roots of the natural life; a cross wherewith God is sometimes pleased to favor His nearest and dearest friends.

And what I say of the patience which you are bound to

practice on all occasions, is to be understood of that portion of any trouble which still remains after we have used all lawful means of relief, and which it is the will of God that we should endure. And in the use of these means we should be guided by the will and disposal of God, Who has appointed them to be used, not to please ourselves, but because He so wills; nor as loving or desiring deliverance from suffering beyond what is required for His service and by His will.

XLII: How to resist the devil when he seeks to delude us by means of indiscreet zeal

When our cunning adversary perceives that we are walking right onward in the path of holiness with fervent yet well-regulated desires, being unable to draw us aside by open allurements, he transforms himself into an angel of light; and by suggestions of seeming friendship, sentences from Scripture, and examples of saints, importunately urges us to aspire indiscreetly to the height of perfection, that so he may cause us to fall headlong from thence. To this end he encourages us to chastise the body with great severity, by fasts, disciplines, hairshirts, and other similar mortifications, that he may either tempt us to pride by the thought that we are doing great things, which is a temptation that especially besets women, or that we may fall sick, and so be disabled from the exercise of good works; or else that from pain and over-weariness we may take a disgust and abhorrence to spiritual exercises, and thus by degrees grow cold in the way of godliness, and at last give ourselves up with greater avidity than before to worldly pleasures and amusements. This has been the end of many, who, following presumptuously the impulse of an indiscreet zeal, have in their excessive outward austerities gone beyond the measure of their interior virtue; and so have perished in their own inventions, and become the sport of malicious ends. This would not have befallen them had they well considered what we have been saying, and remembered that these acts of painful self-discipline, praiseworthy as they are and pro table to such as have corresponding strength of body and humility of spirit, must yet be proportioned to each man's state and condition.

And those who are unequal to labor with the saints in similar austerities, may find other opportunities of imitating their lives by strong and effectual desires and fervent prayers, aspiring after the most glorious crown of Christ's true soldier by despising the whole world and themselves also; by giving themselves up to solitude and silence; by meekness and humility towards all men; by patience under wrongs; by doing good to those most opposed to them; and by avoiding every fault, however trivial it may be; things far more acceptable to God than painful bodily exercises. With regard to these, I would have you to be rather discreetly sparing, in order to be able, if necessary, to increase them, than by certain excesses of zeal to run the risk of having to relinquish them altogether. I say this to you, being well assured you are not likely to fall into the error of those who, though they pass for spiritual, are enticed and deluded by deceitful nature into an over-anxious care for the preservation of their bodily health. So jealous are they, and fearful of the slightest thing which might affect it, that they live in constant doubt and fear of losing it. There is nothing of which they better love to think and speak than of the ordering of their lives in this respect. Hence they are ever solicitous to have food suited rather to their palate than their stomach, which is often weakened by over-delicacy. And though all this is done on the pretext of gaining strength the bet- ter to serve God, it is in fact but a vain attempt to conciliate two mortal enemies, the spirit and the flesh; an attempt which injures both instead of benefiting either; for this same over-carefulness impairs the health of the one and the devotion of the other.

A certain degree of freedom in our way of life is therefore safer and more pro table; accompanied, however, by the discretion of which I have spoken, having regard to different constitutions and states of life, which cannot all be brought under the same rule. In the pursuit of interior holiness, as well as of exterior devotion, we should proceed with moderation, as has been shown before on the subject of the gradual acquisition of virtues.

XLIII: Of the temptation to form rash judgments of our neighbor, arising from the instigation of the Devil and the strength of our own evil inclinations, and of the way to resist this temptation

From this same vice of self-esteem and self-conceit arises another most injurious to us, i.e. rash judgment of our neighbor, leading us to despise, contemn, and disparage him. And this fault, which arises from our pride and evil inclination, is by the same pride voluntarily nourished and increased; for as it increases, so does pride also increase, insensibly flattering and deluding us.

For the more we presume to exalt ourselves, the more do we un- consciously depress others; while we imagine ourselves free from those imperfections which we think we perceive in them.

And the cunning tempter, who discovers this most evil disposition in us, is continually on the watch to open our eyes and keep them awake to see, investigate, and exaggerate the defects of other men. Careless souls know not and believe not how diligently he studies and contrives to impress upon our minds the little failings of this or that person, when he cannot discover to us greater faults.

Therefore, as he is watching to do you hurt, be you also awake, lest you fall into his snare. And when he brings before you any defect of your neighbor, banish the thought at once; and if you still feel a temptation to pass judgment upon it, resist the impulse. Consider that the office of judge has not been committed to thee; and that even if it were, beset as you are by a thousand passions, and but too prone to think evil without just cause, you would be unable to form a righteous judgment.

And, as an effectual remedy against rash judgments, I would remind you to occupy your thoughts with your own defects; so will you perceive more and more plainly every hour how much you have to do in yourself and for yourself, and will find neither time nor inclination to attend to the doings of others.

Besides, by faithfully performing this exercise you will be en abled more and more to purge your inward sight from the malignant humors whence this pestilent vice proceeds.

And know, that whenever you are so unhappy as to think any evil of your brother, then is some root of the same evil in your own heart; which, in proportion as it is ill-disposed itself, gives a ready welcome to anything like itself.

Whenever, therefore, it comes into your mind to judge another for some fault, despise your own self as guilty of the same, and say in your heart, "How can a wretch like me, laden with this and far worse faults, dare to lift up my head to see and judge the faults of others!"

And thus will the weapon, which, directed against another, would have wounded you, being turned against thyself, bring healing to your wounds.

If the error committed be clear and manifest, find some com- passionate excuse for it, and believe that in your brother are some hidden virtues, for the sake of which the Lord has suffered him to fall, or to be for some time subject to this failing, that he may become vile in his own sight; and that, being also despised by others on this account, he may reap the fruit of humiliation, and render himself more acceptable to God, and so his gain may become greater than his loss.

But if the sin be not only manifest, but grievous and willfully obstinate, turn your thoughts upon God's awful judgments. Then you will see men who were once great sinners attaining high degrees of sanctity; and others, who seemed to have reached the most sublime heights of perfection, falling into the lowest depths of perdition.

Therefore fear and tremble for yourself far more than for any other.

And be assured, that every good and kindly feeling towards your neighbor is the gift of the Holy Ghost; and that all rash judgment, all contempt and bitterness towards him, flow from our own evil hearts and the suggestions of Satan.

If, then, any imperfection of another have made an impression on your mind, rest not nor give slumber to your eyes until to the utmost of your power you have effaced it from your heart.

The Fourth Weapon of the Spiritual Combat

XLIV: On prayer

If self-distrust, trust in God, and spiritual exercises, be so needful, as has been already shown, in this conflict, needful above all is prayer (the fourth weapon above mentioned) by means of which we may obtain from the Lord our God not these alone, but all other good things.

Prayer is the instrument for obtaining all the graces which flow down upon us from that Divine Source of love and goodness. By prayer, well used, you will put a sword into the hand of God wherewith to fight and conquer for you.

And to use it well, you must be well exercised in the following practices, or be striving to become so.

1.   You must have an earnest desire to serve His Divine Majesty in all things, in the way most acceptable to Him.

In order to enkindle this desire, consider well that God is supremely worthy to be served and honored for His supreme excellencies, His wisdom, goodness, majesty, beauty, and all His other infinite perfections. That to serve you He labored and suffered for three-and-thirty years; binding up and healing the putrefying sores envenomed by the poison of sin, not with oil, or wine, or linen, but with the precious stream that owed from His most sacred veins, and with His most pure flesh torn by scourges, thorns, and nails.

And consider further the great value of this service. By it we gain the mastery over Satan and ourselves, and are made the children of God Himself.

2. You must have a lively faith and confidence that the Lord will give you all things needful for His service and your good.

This holy confidence is the vessel which Divine Mercy fills with the treasures of His grace; and the larger and more capacious it is, the more richly laden will our prayer return into our bosom. For how shall the almighty and unchanging God fail to impart to us His gifts, when He has Himself commanded us to ask for them; promising, also, to give us His Spirit, if we ask with faith and perseverance?

3. When you pray, let it be your intention to will God's will alone, and not your own, as well in asking as in obtaining; that is, pray because God wills you to pray, and desire to be heard in so far and no farther than He wills. Your intention, in short, should be to unite your will to the will of God, and not to draw His will to yours.

And this because your will, being infected and ruined by self-love, often errs, and knows not what to ask; but the Divine Will, being always united to fine able goodness, can never err.

The will of God is therefore the rule and ruler of all other wills; and it deserves and wills to be followed and obeyed by all.

Ask, therefore, always such things as are conformable to God's will; and if you be in doubt whether anything be so or not, ask it on the condition of its being according to the will of God.

And those things (such as all virtues) which you certainly know to be agreeable to Him, ask rather in order to serve and please Him thereby than for any other motive, how spiritual so-ever.

4. Be careful when you go to prayer to adorn yourself with works corresponding to your petitions; and after you have prayed, labor more earnestly still to fit yourself for the grace and virtue you desire to obtain.

For the exercise of prayer must be so continually accompanied by the exercise of self-discipline, that the one may involve the other; else, to pray for a virtue and take no trouble to obtain it, would be rather to tempt God than to serve Him.

5.   Let your petitions be ordinarily preceded by thanksgiving for previous mercies, in the following or similar forms:

"O Lord, Who of your goodness have created and redeemed me, and on so many and numberless occasions, unknown to me, have delivered me out of the hands of my enemies; help me now, and refuse not my petitions, though I have been ever rebellious and ungrateful to you."

And if, while you are praying for any particular virtue, some painful occasion for its exercise should present itself, fail not to return thanks to God for the opportunity thus afforded you, which is no small token of His loving-kindness.

6.   As prayer derives its efficacy and its power of propitiating God and inclining Him to our desires from the goodness and mercifulness of His own nature, from the merits of the life and passion of His only-begotten Son, and from His promise to hear us, conclude your petitions with one or more of the following sentences:

"Of your great mercy, O Lord, grant me your grace. May the merits of your Son obtain for me my petition. Remember Your promises, O my God, and incline Your ear to my prayer."

And at other times ask for graces through the merits of the Virgin Mary and the Saints, who have great power with God, and are greatly honored by Him, because in this life they greatly honored His Divine Majesty.

Continue perseveringly in prayer; for humble perseverance vanquishes the invincible. And, if the importunity of the widow in the Gospel inclined to her request the unjust judge laden with iniquity, shall a like perseverance fail to incline to our petitions that God Who is Himself the plenitude of goodness?

And although the Lord should delay to hear, and even seem to reject your prayer, pray on still, and still hold fast firm and lively confidence in His aid; for in Him there is no lack, but an infinite superabundance of all things needful for the grace we ask.

Therefore, unless there be some fault on your part, you may rest assured either of obtaining all your petition, or something which will be more pro table for you, or, it may be, both together; and the more He seems to repulse you, the more do you humble yourself in your own sight, considering your own demerits, and fixing your eyes steadfastly on the mercy of God. Establish thus more and more your confidence in Him, which will be most acceptable to your Lord, if you maintain it more lively and entire the more it is assailed. Lastly, give thanks always to God, acknowledging Him to be no less good, and wise, and loving, when some things are denied, than if all were granted you. Happen what may, do you remain ever steadfast and joyful in humble submission to His Divine Providence.

XLV: Mental prayer

Mental Prayer is the elevation of our minds to God, asking of Him either expressly or tacitly those things of which we stand in need. We ask for them expressly when we say in our hearts: "O my God, grant me this request for the honor of Thy holy name"; or "Lord, I am firmly convinced that this petition is Thy will, and for Thy greater honor, I ask this petition. Accomplish, therefore, Thy Divine will in me."

When harassed by the attacks of the enemy, let us say: "Come swiftly, O Lord, to my assistance lest I fall a prey to my enemy"; or "O God, my refuge and my strength, help me speedily, lest I perish." When temptation continues, we must continue the same prayer, courageously resisting the foe; and when the fury of the combat has passed, let us address ourselves to the Almighty, imploring Him to consider our weakness in the face of the enemy's strength: "Behold, my God, Thy creature, the work of Thy hands, a man redeemed by Thy precious blood. And behold Satan trying to carry him from Thee to utterly destroy him. It is to Thee I fly for aid, and it is in Thee that I place my entire confidence, for I know that Thou alone art infinitely good and powerful. Have pity on a miserable creature who stumbles blindly, though willfully, into the path of his enemies, as do all who forsake the assistance of Thy grace. Help me therefore, my only hope, O sole strength of my soul!"

We tacitly ask favors of God when we present to Him our necessities, without making any particular request. Placing ourselves in His Divine presence, we acknowledge our incapacity to avoid evil or do good without His aid. We are nevertheless inflamed with a desire of serving Him. Thus we must fix our eyes upon Him, waiting for His assistance with unbounded confidence and utter humility.

The confession of our weakness and the desire to serve Him, this act of faith so performed, is a silent prayer which will infallibly obtain our request from Heaven. The more sincere the confession, the more ardent the desire, and the more lively the faith, the greater will be the efficacy of the prayer before the throne of God.

There is another method of prayer similar to this, but more concise, consisting as it does in but a single act of the soul. The soul presents her requests to the Almighty, adverting to a favor already asked and still sought, although not formally expressed.

Let us endeavor to cultivate this kind of prayer, and employ it on all occasions; for experience will convince us that nothing is more easy, yet nothing more excellent and efficacious.

XLVI: Meditation

When a considerable length of time [as a half-hour, hour, or an even longer period] is to be spent in prayer, it is advisable to make a meditation on some feature of our Savior's life or passion; the reflections naturally arising from such meditation should then be applied to the particular virtue we are striving to attain.

If, for instance, you need patience, contemplate the mystery of your Savior scourged at the pillar. Consider first the blows and revilements hurled at Him by the soldiers as they brutally drag their innocent victim to the appointed place as ordered. Secondly, consider Him stripped of His garments, exposed to the piercing cold. Thirdly, picture those innocent hands, bound tightly to the pillar. Fourthly, consider His body, torn with whips until His blood moistened the earth. And finally, envision the frequency of the blows, creating new wounds, reopening others on that sacred body.

Dwelling on these or similar details, calculated to inspire in you a love of patience, you should try to feel within your very soul the inexpressible anguish so patiently borne by your Divine Master. Then consider the excruciating agony of His spirit, and the patience and mildness with which that agony was endured by Him Who was ready to suffer even more for God's glory and your welfare.

Behold, then, your Master, covered with blood, desiring nothing more earnestly than your patient acceptance of affliction; and be assured that He implores for you the assistance of the Heavenly Father that you may bear with resignation, not only the cross of the moment, but the crosses to come. Strengthen, therefore, by frequent acts your resolution to suffer, with joy; and, raising your mind to Heaven, give thanks to the Father of mercies, Who didst send His only Son into this world to suffer indescribable torments, and to intercede for you in your necessities.

Conclude your meditation by beseeching Him to grant you

the virtue of patience, through the merits and intercession of this beloved Son in Whom He is well pleased.

XLVII: Another Method of Meditation

There is another method of prayer and meditation besides the one to which we have adverted. In this latter method, having considered the poignant sufferings of your Savior and His patient endurance of them, you proceed to two other considerations of equal importance.

The one is the consideration of Christ's infinite merits, and the other, of that satisfaction and glory which the eternal Father received from His obedience – an obedience unto death, even the death of the Cross.

You must represent these two considerations to the Divine Majesty, as two powerful means of obtaining the grace you seek. This method is applicable, not only to all the mysteries of Our Lord's passion, but to every exterior or interior act He performed in the course of His passion

XLVIII: A Method of Prayer based on the Intercession of the Blessed Virgin

Besides the methods of meditation already mentioned, there is another which is addressed particularly to the Blessed Virgin. We first consider the eternal Father, then Jesus Christ Our Lord, and finally, the Blessed Mother.

With regard to the eternal Father, there are two considerations. The first is the singular affection He cherished from all eternity for this most chaste Virgin whom He chose to be the mother of His Divine Son. The second is the eminent sanctity He was pleased to bestow upon her and the many virtues she practiced in her lifetime.

Meditating on the affection of the eternal Father for our Lady, you must begin by raising your mind above all created beings; look forward to the vast expanses of eternity, enter into the heart of God, and see with what delight He viewed the person destined one day to become the mother of His Son; beseech Him by that delight to give you sufficient strength against your enemies, especially those who most grievously afflict you. Contemplate, then, the virtues and heroic actions of this incomparable Virgin; make an offering of each or all of them to God, as they are of such efficacy as to obtain for you divine assistance in your particular necessities.

After this address yourself to Jesus, begging Him to be mindful of that loving mother who for nine months carried Him in her womb, and from the moment of His birth paid Him the most profound adoration. For this was her acknowledgment that this Child was at once God and man, her Creator and her Son. With compassion she saw Him poorly accommodated in a humble stable, nourished Him with her pure milk, kissed and embraced Him a thousand times with maternal fondness, and through His life and at His death, suffered for Him beyond expression. Present this picture to the Savior, that He may be compelled, as it were, by such powerful motives, to hear your prayers.

Appeal to the Blessed Virgin herself, reminding her of her commission from all eternity, to be the Mother of Mercy and the refuge of sinners, and that after her divine Son, you place your greatest confidence in her intercession. Present to her the fact, asserted by the learned and confirmed by miracles, that no one ever called upon her with a lively faith, and was left unaided.

Finally, remind her of the sufferings of her Son for your salvation, that she may obtain of Him the grace necessary to make proper use of His sufferings for the greater glory of that loving Savior.

XLIX: Some Considerations to induce Confidence in the Assistance of the Blessed Virgin

Whoever wishes to have recourse to the Blessed Virgin confidently must observe the following motives.

1. Experience teaches us that a vessel which has contained perfumes preserves their odor, especially if the perfume is in the container for any length of time, or if any remain in it; yet here there is but a limited power, similar to the warmth carried from a re, the source of that warmth.

If such be the case, what are we to say of the charity and compassion of the Blessed Virgin, who for nine months bore, and still carries in her heart, the only Son of God, the uncreated charity which knows no bounds? If, as often as we approach a fire, we are affected by its heat, have we not reason to believe that whoever approaches the heart of the Mother of Mercies, ever burning with her most ardent charity, must be profoundly affected in proportion to the frequency of his petitions, the humility and confidence in his heart?

2. No creature ever loved Jesus Christ more ardently, nor showed more perfect submission to His will, than Mary, His mother. If then, this Savior, immolated for us sinners, gave His mother to us, an advocate and intercessor for all time, she cannot but comply with His request, and will not refuse us her assistance. Let us, then, not hesitate to implore her pity; let us have recourse to her with great confidence in all our necessities, as she is an inexhaustible source of blessings, bestowing her favors in proportion to the confidence placed in her.

L: A Method of Meditation and Prayer involving the Intercession of the Saints and the Angels

The following methods of obtaining the protection of the saints and angels may be employed.

The first method is to address yourself to the eternal Father, laying before Him the hymns of Heavenly choirs, the labors, persecutions, and torments suffered by the Saints on earth for love of Him. Then, in recalling their fidelity and love, beseech Him to grant your petitions.

The second method is to invoke the Angels, those blessed spirits earnestly desirous, not only of our earthly perfection, but of our greater Heavenly perfection. Earnestly beseech them to assist you in subduing your evil inclinations and conquering the enemies of your salvation; and beg a particular remembrance at the hour of death.

Sometimes think over the extraordinary graces God has granted to the Saints and Angels, and rejoice as if they had been bestowed on yourself. Rather, let your joy be even greater for His having bestowed such favors on them rather than on yourself, for such was His will; and you should bless and praise God in the accomplishment of His Divine plan.

To facilitate the regularity and performance of this exercise, it would be well to assign the different days of the week to the different orders of the blessed. On Sunday, implore the intercession of the nine Angelic choirs; on Monday, invoke John the Baptist; on Tuesday, the patriarchs and prophets; on Wednesday, the Apostles; on Thursday, the Martyrs; on Friday, bishops and confessors; on Saturday, the virgins and other Saints. But let no day pass without imploring the assistance of Our Lady, the queen of all the Saints, your guardian Angel, the glorious Archangel St. Michael, or any other saint to whom you have any particular devotion.

Moreover, beseech daily the eternal Father, His Divine Son, and the Blessed Virgin, that you may be particularly under the protection of St. Joseph, the worthy spouse of the most chaste of virgins. Then addressing yourself to this loving protector, ask with great humility to be received into his care. For innumerable are the instances of assistance afforded to those who have called upon St. Joseph in their spiritual or temporal necessities. Particularly has he aided them when they stood in need of light from heaven, and direction in their prayers. And if God shows so much regard for the other saints who have loved and served Him here below, how much consideration and deference will He not show for the person He so honored as to pay him filial homage and obedience?

LI: Meditation on the Sufferings of Christ and the Sentiments to be derived from Contemplation of them

What I prescribed previously concerning the method of praying and meditating on the sufferings of our Lord and Savior regarded only the petition of those things of which we stand in need; now we are to proceed to the adoption of the proper sentiments from our considerations. For instance, if you have chosen the crucifixion and its attendant circumstances as the subject of your meditation, you may dwell on the following considerations. Consider first the arrival of Jesus on Mount Calvary. His executioners rudely stripped Him, tearing o the garments which adhered to the torn flesh of His lacerated body. Consider next the fresh wounds made in His Sacred Head by the crown of thorns, removed and reset by his barbarous executioners. Next, visualize Him nailed to the cross with spikes, driven through the flesh and wood with a large hammer. Consider that His hands, not reaching the places designed for them, were stretched so violently that all His bones were disjointed, enabling the onlooker to count His very bones [Psalm XXL, 18]. Then think of the actual elevation of the cross, and the weight of Christ's body resting on nails which tore gaping wounds in His hands and feet, giving Him excruciating pain.

If, by these and similar considerations you wish to enkindle the flames of Divine love within your heart, try to attain by meditation a sublime knowledge of the infinite goodness of your Savior, Who for you condescended to suffer so much. For the more you advance in the knowledge of His love for you, the greater will be your love and affection for Him. Being convinced of His extraordinary charity, you will naturally conceive a sincere sorrow for having so often and so heinously offended Him, Who offered Himself as a sacrifice for your offenses.

Proceed then to make acts of hope, considering that this great God on the Cross had no other plan than to extirpate sin from the world, to free you from the devil, to expiate your crimes, to reconcile you to His Father, and to provide a resource for you in all your necessities. But if, after contemplating His passion, you consider its effects, your sorrow will be turned into joy. For observe that by Christ's death the sins of humanity were blotted out, the anger of a sovereign Judge appeased, the powers of Hell defeated, death itself vanquished, and the places of the fallen Angels filled in Heaven. And the joy arising from such reflection will be increased by thinking of the joy with which the Holy Trinity, the Blessed Virgin, the church militant and triumphant received the glad, tidings of the redemption of mankind.

If you would have a lively sorrow for your sins, let your meditation convince you that if Jesus Christ suffered so much, it was to inspire you with wholesome self-contempt, and a hatred of your disorderly passions, particularly your greatest faults, which are naturally most offensive to Almighty God.

And if you would excite sentiments of admiration, you need only consider that nothing is more shocking than the sight of the Creator of the universe, the fountain of life, butchered by His own creatures, the right of the supreme majesty, as it were, annihilated, justice condemned, beauty de led and lost in filth, the beloved of the Eternal Father become the hated of sinners. Light inaccessible is overwhelmed by the powers of darkness; uncreated glory and felicity are buried under ignominy and wretchedness.

To arouse compassion in your heart for the sufferings of your Savior and God, exclusive of His exterior pains, consider the most acute of His sufferings, His interior anguish. For if you are moved by the first, you will be pierced with grief at the sight of the second. The soul of Christ beheld the Divinity then as clearly as it does now in heaven. It knew how much God deserved to be honored, and as it infinitely loved Him, desired that all creatures should love Him with all the power of their souls. Seeing Him, therefore, so horribly dishonored throughout the world by countless, abominable crimes, it was overwhelmed with grief that the Divine majesty was not loved and served by all men. As the greatness of this desire of the soul of Christ that His Father be loved was beyond imagination, it is futile to try to comprehend the depths of His interior sufferings in the agonies of death.

Moreover, as this Divine Savior loved mankind to an ineffable degree, such an ardent and tender love must have caused Him much sorrow for the sins that would tear men from Him. For He knew that no one could sin mortally without destroying that sanctifying grace which is the bond between Him and the just. And this separation would cause Jesus greater anguish of soul than dislocated limbs caused His body. For the soul, altogether spiritual and immeasurably superior to the body, is much more delicately attuned to pain. But of all the afflictions of our blessed Savior, the most grievous, doubtless, was the sight of the damned, incapable of repentance, who must inevitably be banished from Him for all eternity.

If the contemplation of such suffering moves you to compassion for your dying Jesus, meditate further, and you will find that His excessive suffering was not caused by your sins alone; for His precious blood was shed not only to cleanse you from the sins you have committed, but to preserve you from those you might have committed were you unaided by Heaven. It is a fact that you will never be without motives for taking part in the sufferings of Jesus crucified. Know, moreover, that human nature never was, and never will be subject to any affliction that was unknown to Him. He suffered from injuries, reproaches, temptations, pains, loss of goods, voluntary austerities more acutely than those who groan under them. For as this tender Savior had a perfect comprehension of any affliction of mind or body to which we are prone even to the least pain or headache He must certainly have been moved with great compassion for us.

Who, however, can express what He felt at the sight of His

Blessed Mother's affliction? For she shared in all the pangs and outrages which attended His passion, and with the same views and from the same motives. And although her sufferings were infinitely short of His, they were excruciating beyond expression. The awareness of our Lady's agony redoubled the sorrows of Jesus, and pierced His heart still deeper. Hence it was that a certain devout soul compared the heart of Jesus to a burning furnace in which He voluntarily suffered from the ardent flames of Divine love.

Arid after all, what is the cause of such unspeakable agony? Nothing but our sins; this is the answer. Therefore, the greatest compassion and gratitude we can possibly show towards Him Who has suffered so much for us, is to be truly sorry for our past offenses out of pure love for Him; to detest sin with all the fervor of our soul because it is displeasing to Him; and to wage ceaseless war against our evil inclinations because they are His greatest enemies. Thus divesting ourselves of the old man, and putting on the new, we adorn our souls with virtue, in which alone their beauty consists.

LII: The Benefits derived from Meditations on the Cross and the Imitation of the Virtue of Christ Crucified

Great are the advantages to be derived from meditating on the Cross, the first of which is, not only a detestation of past sins, but also the firm resolution to fight against our ever present disorderly appetites, which crucified our Savior. The second advantage is the forgiveness of sins, obtained from Jesus crucified, and a wholesome self-contempt which inspires us forever to forsake o ending Him, and continually to love and serve Him with all our hearts in acknowledgment of what He suffered for our sakes. The third is the unceasing labor with which we root out all depraved habits, however trivial they may appear. The fourth consists in our ardent e orts to imitate our Divine Master, Who died, not only to expiate our sins, but to bequeath to us the sublime example of a life of sanctity and perfection.

The following method of meditation will be highly serviceable, assuming as I do, that you particularly wish to imitate the patience of your Savior in carrying your crosses. Consider well these several points:

- ❖ What the soul of Christ suffered for God. What God did for the soul of Jesus.
- ❖ What the soul of Jesus did for itself and its body. What Jesus did for us.
- ❖ What we ought to do for Jesus.

1. Consider in the first place, that the soul of Jesus engulfed in the ocean of Divinity, contemplated that infinite and incomprehensible Being, before Whom even the most exalted of creatures is utterly insignificant; contemplated, I say, in a state so debased as to suffer the vilest indignities of ungrateful man, without the least diminution of its essential glory and splendor. And from the depths of its suffering, the soul of Christ adored its sovereign Majesty, giving it myriad thanks and accepting all for its sake.

2. Behold on the other hand what God bestowed on the soul of Jesus; consider that the Divine will decreed the scourgings, spittle, blasphemies, buffetings, crown of thorns for love of us, and the crucifixion, which were meted out to Jesus, the only and beloved Son of God. See with what delight God, knowing the admirable end to which it was all directed, beheld His Divine Son, loaded with infamy and overwhelmed with affliction.

3. Contemplate next the soul of Jesus, and observe with what alacrity it submitted itself to the will of God, either because of the immensity of its Divine perfection, or the infinity of divine favor bestowed upon it. Who can describe the ardent affection of this soul for crosses? This was a soul that sought even new ways of suffering, and failing in this, abandoned itself and the innocent body to the mercy of miscreants and the

powers of Hell.

4. Turn, then, your eyes to Jesus, Who from the midst of His agony, addresses you in this affectionate manner: "See to what depths of misery I am reduced by thy ungovernable will, which refuses the least constraint in compliance with mine. Behold the horrible pains I endure, with no other purpose than to teach thee a lesson of patience. And let me persuade thee, by all these sufferings, to accept with resignation this cross I here present, and those which I shall send in the future. Surrender thy reputation to calumny, and thy body to the fury of the persecutors whom I shall choose for thy trial, however vile and inhuman they may be. Oh, that thou didst know what delight thy patience and resignation afford me! But then, how canst thou be ignorant of it, when thou beholdest these wounds received to purchase for thee those virtues with which I would adorn thy soul, more dear to me than life itself? If I have suffered this debasement for thee, canst thou not bear a light affliction, in order to lessen My agony to some degree? Canst thou refuse to heal those wounds I have received through thy impatience, wounds more cruel to me than physical anguish?"

5. Consider who it is that speaks thus to you; consider that it is Jesus Christ, the King of Glory, true God and true Man. Consider too the magnitude of His torments and humiliations, greater than that deserved by the most vicious of criminals. Be astonished to behold Him in the midst of these agonies, not only firm and resolute, but even replenished with joy, as if the day of His passion was a day of triumph. Just as a few drops of water sprinkled upon a flame only adds a fresh intensity to its glow, so did His torments, embraced in a charity which made the burden seem light, serve to augment his joy and desire of suffering still greater affliction.

Moreover, reflect that throughout His entire life, He was motivated, not by compulsion or self-interest, but rather by pure love alone, that you may learn from Him the manner of practicing patience. Endeavor, therefore, to attain a perfect knowledge of what He demands of you, and consider His delight at your practice of patience. Then form an ardent desire of carrying this cross and heavier ones, not only with patience, but with joy, that you may more exactly imitate Christ crucified and render yourself more acceptable to Him.

Picture to ourself all the torments and indignities of His passion, and amazed at His constancy, blush at your own weakness. Look upon your sufferings as merely imaginative when compared to His, and regard your patience as not even the faintest shadow of His. Dread nothing so much as an unwillingness to suffer for your Savior, rejecting such unwillingness as a suggestion from Hell.

Consider Jesus on the Cross as you would a devout book worthy of your unceasing study and by which you may learn the practice of the most heroic virtues. This is the book which may be truly called the "Book of Life" [Apocalypse, III, 5], which at once enlightens the mind by its doctrines and inflames the will by its examples. The world is full of books, but were it possible for man to read them all, he would never be so well instructed to hate vice and embrace virtue as by contemplating a crucified God. But remember that there are those who spend hours lamenting the passion of our Lord and admiring His patience, and yet on the first occasion betray as great an impatience in suffering as if they had never thought of the cross. Such men are like untried soldiers, who in their barracks breathe nothing but conquest, but on the first appearance of the enemy, beat a hasty and inglorious retreat. What is more despicable after considering, admiring and extolling the virtues of our Redeemer, than to forget them all in an instant when an opportunity of practicing them presents itself?

Communion

LIII: Concerning the most Holy Sacrament of the Eucharist

Thus far, I have tried, as perhaps you have observed, to furnish you with four kinds of spiritual weapons, and the methods by which they may be profitably employed; it remains to present to you the invaluable aids to be derived from the Holy Eucharist in subduing the enemies of perfection and salvation. As this sublime Sacrament towers above the others in dignity and efficacy, it is the most terrible of all weapons to the infernal powers.

The methods previously treated have no force but through the merits of Jesus Christ, and by the grace He has purchased for us by His Precious Blood; but the Eucharist is Jesus Christ Himself, His Body, His Blood, His Soul and Divinity. The former methods are bestowed upon us by God that we may use them in subduing the enemy through Jesus Christ; but the Eucharist is given that we may fight against the enemy with Him. For by eating the Body of Jesus, and drinking His Blood we dwell in Him and He in us. We may eat His Body and drink His Blood in reality every day, and spiritually every hour, both of which are highly profitable and holy. The latter should be practiced as often as possible, the former as often as shall be judged expedient.

LIV: The manner in which we ought to receive the Blessed Sacrament

The motives for approaching this Divine Sacrament are many, from which it follows that there are various requirements to be observed at three different times:

❖ Before Communion
❖ At the moment of reception of Communion
❖ After Communion

1. **Before Communion**, whatever be our motive, we must, if stained with mortal sin, cleanse ourselves in the sacrament of Penance. And with all sincerity of heart, we must offer ourselves to Jesus Christ, consecrating our souls and all their faculties to His service. For it is in this Sacrament that He bestows to mankind His Body, Blood, Soul, and Divinity, together with the immense and inexhaustible treasure of His infinite merits. And as all of our gifts to Him are insignificant when compared to His gifts to us, we should desire nothing less than the totality of merits gained by the created beings of the universe to offer as a present deserving His regard.

If our desire is victory over spiritual adversaries, we should meditate for some time previous to the reception of Communion on the incomprehensibly ardent desire of our Savior to be one with us in suppressing our inordinate appetites.

In order, however, to formulate some idea of this Divine wish in our regard, we might consider two things. The first is the ineffable joy with which wisdom incarnate dwells among us, for He calls it His delight [Prov. VIII, 31]. The second is the implacable hatred He bears toward mortal sin, inasmuch as it is both an insuperable obstacle to that much-desired intimate union with Him, and in utter opposition to His Divine perfections. For as God is sovereignly good, a light undimmed and beauty inviolate, He must inevitably hate sin which is all malice, all darkness, and all corruption. So burning indeed is this hatred of God for sin, that the entire dispensation of the Old and New Testaments has been ordained for its destruction. Several of God's saints have said that divinity would have suffered a thousand deaths on a thousand Golgothas if the smallest faults could be annihilated within us.

These considerations, rudimentary as they are, may enable you to see how much our Savior desires to dwell within our hearts to expiate therefrom our common enemies; thus we should welcome Him with all the fervor of which we are capable. The joyful expectancy of His arrival will raise our courage, and inspire us to war anew on our predominant passion by performing many acts of the contrary virtue. Particularly should this be so on the evening before and on the morning of our reception of Holy Communion.

2. When we are about to receive the body of Our Lord, let us quickly consider the faults committed since our last communion, and in order to conceive a more perfect sorrow, let us remember that we committed them as callously as if Christ had not died for us on Calvary's tree. Such a remembrance should fill us with shame and fear for having basely preferred a trifling compliance to our own will to the obedience due so gracious a master. But when we consider that in spite of this ingratitude and in fidelity, this God of all charity still condescends to visit us and live within us, then let us approach Him with confidence and open hearts; for when He lives within, no tainted affections of the world may steal in.

3. After Communion, we are to remain in profound recollection, adoring Our Lord with great humility and saying within our souls: "Thou seest, O God of my soul, my wretched propensity to sin; Thou seest how domineering is this passion, and that of myself I cannot resist. It is Thou Who must fight my battles, and if I share in the combat, it is Thee from Whom I must expect the crown of victory!"

Then addressing ourselves to the Eternal Father, let us offer to Him this beloved Son Who now dwells within our breast; let us offer Him thanks for innumerable benefits and implore Him for the grace that will make our victory complete.

Finally, let us resolve to fight courageously against the enemy from whom we suffer most. Thus we may expect victory, since if we are not wanting in petition, God is not wanting in bestowing, and sooner or later victory will be ours.

LV: Preparation for Communion and the role of the Eucharist in exciting in us a Love of God

If our motive in receiving Holy Communion be a desire of increasing our love of God, we should recall the love which God has for us. The preparation consists in an attentive contemplation of this Sovereign Lord of boundless power and majesty, Who not satisfied with creating us to His image and likeness, nor with the immolation of His only Son in our behalf, left this Son to us in the Sacrament of the Eucharist to be our food and support in all our necessities. Consider well the greatness and uniqueness of this love in the following manner:

1. In its duration we find that God's love for us is eternal and unceasing; for as He is eternal in His Divinity, so is He eternal in His love. Before time was, God determined to give His Son to mankind in this marvelous manner. Let these words, then, echo joyfully within your heart: "In the abyss of eternity, my littleness was so loved by the most high God, that He thought of me, and with love fine able wished to give me His Son to be my food and my nourishment!"

2. Our strongest passions for earthly things recognize certain limits which they cannot exceed, but the love of God for us is limitless. The advent of His Son, equal to Him in majesty and perfection, was a testimony to that boundless love. Thus is the gift equal to the love, and the love to the gift; and both are infinite, beyond the borders of human understanding.

3. In loving us God was not constrained by any power or necessity, but heaped innumerable benefits upon us out of the magnitude of Divine love.

4. Neither have human merit or previous good works rendered us worthy of this remarkable gift. If God has loved to

excess or given of Himself unstintingly, it is rather to be attributed to the immensity of Divine charity.

5.   God's love for us is untainted with the blemish of the self-interest present in human affections. For what is the totality of human greatness to Him, the source of all happiness and glory? How could we possibly add glory to glory itself? The advantages, then, are all on the side of man.

Meditating on this truth, let each man say within himself: "Who could have imagined, O Lord, that a God of such infinite greatness would bestow His affections on such an abject and insignificant creature as myself! What could be Thy design, O King of glory? What canst Thou expect of me who am but dust? I see clearly, O my God, by the light of Thy burning charity which enlightens me with knowledge and enkindles me with love, that Thy design was one divorced from all self-interest. For Thy wish in so graciously bestowing this sacrament is to transform me into Thee, that I may live in Thee and Thou in me. Such an intimate union will ultimately remake my heart, fashioning from a vessel of earth, a delicate instrument attuned to things Divine."

Then, full of joy and wonder at the indications of Divine love given us by Christ, and aware that His only purpose is the trans- formation of our hearts from things of earth to things of heaven, let us offer a sacrifice, and consecrate the will, the memory, and understanding to the sole task of pleasing Him in the gracious acceptance of His holy will. After this, recognizing our incapacity to dispose ourselves properly, unaided by His grace for proper reception of the Eucharist, let us strive earnestly to obtain that grace by ejaculations such as the following:

"O heavenly food, when shall I be united to Thee, to be consumed joyfully in the re of Divine love? O Divine charity, when shall I live in Thee, by Thee, and for Thee alone? O heavenly manna, sovereign good, joy of my heart, when shall I, loathing all other food, seek Thee alone? O life of eternal joy, when shall I dwell in Thee alone? O my loving and almighty Lord, free my heart from the tyranny of its passions and vicious attachments; adorn it with Thy heavenly virtues, and with gentle compulsion force it to rejoice in loving and pleasing Thee. Then O Lord, will I open my heart and bid Thee enter; then shalt Thou come, my only treasure, to transform my heart by Thy Divine presence."

Such are the tender and affectionate sentiments which we should form on the evening before, and on the morning of reception of Holy Communion.

When the time itself draws near, we must consider attentively who it is that we are about to receive; for our guest is to be the Son of the living God, the august majesty before Whom the heavens and the powers of Heaven tremble in awesome fear. Our guest is to be the Saint of Saints, mirror without blemish, purity itself, before Whom all is unclean in comparison. This is Divinity become man; one looked upon as the very outcast of men, Who was pleased to be spat upon, struck, reviled, and crucified out of love for us. You are indeed about to receive God Himself, in Whose hand is the destiny of the universe.

On the other hand, think of your own utter insignificance, and your vile sinfulness which has reduced you below the level of the brute, and made you worthy of being the sport and slave of devils. Consider your acknowledgment of the infinite favors you have received from your Savior; you have insulted the Redeemer and trampled upon His Precious Blood, displaying a most arrant ingratitude.

But even human ingratitude cannot overcome divine charity; capricious fickleness is no match for unchanging love. Still the gracious Lord summons you to the Divine banquet, and rather than rebuffing you for your obvious inadequacies, bids you come under pain of death. The arms of the merciful Father are always open to receive you, be you leprous, lame, blind, profligate, or possessed by devils. He demands of you these few requisites alone:

❖ To be sincerely sorry for having so grievously o ended

Him. To hate sin of all kind with an unquenchable vigor.

❖ To consecrate yourself to cheerful acceptance of His Divine will whatever it may be.

❖ To have a firm confidence that He will forgive your sins, cleanse your soul of all taint, and defend you against all your enemies.

Encouraged by this ineffable love of the Lord for you and all penitent sinners, approach the holy table with a prudent fear, tempered by hope and love, saying:

"After so many grievous offenses, I am not worthy to receive Thee, not having fully satisfied Thy justice. No, my God, I am unworthy of Thee, sullied as I am by an inordinate attachment to creatures and a reluctance to serve Thee completely with my whole heart and my whole strength.

O my omnipotent Lord, be mindful of Thy goodness and Thy promise; through the Divine alchemy of love and faith, make my heart a worthy dwelling place for Thy Divine Son."

After Communion strive to be deeply recollected, shutting out from your heart the multiple petty encroachments of worldly distractions. Entertain the Divine guest with such sentiments as are expressed in the following prayer:

"O sovereign Lord of Heaven, what has brought Thee from celestial heights to the depths of earthly hearts?" His answer will be simply, "Love."

And you must reply: "O eternal love, what is it you ask of me?" And He will answer again: "Nothing but love. I would have no other re within thee but charity, the ardent flames of which will conquer the impure flames of passion, and make thee pleasing in My sight."

"Long have I wished that thou wert all Mine, and I all thine. And long have I desired that surrender of thy will ever solicitous for frivolous liberty and worldly vanities; for only when thy will is attuned to Mine can the first wish be realized."

"Know, then, that I would have thee die to self, that you might live to Me; I would have thee give Me thy heart that I might make it like unto Mine, which broke on Calvary out of love for mankind. Thou knowest who I am, and yet thou knowest that in some measure, I have made thee My equal in an excess of love. When I give Myself entirely to thee, I ask nothing but thyself in return. Be Mine and I shall be satisfied. Will nothing, think nothing, understand nothing, see nothing but Me and My will. Let thy nothingness be lost in the depths of My infinity, and find there thy happiness, as I find repose in thee."

Finally offer to the Eternal Father His Only-begotten Son:
First in thanksgiving for the unspeakably great favors He has rendered in bestowing them on you.
In petition for such things as are needed by you and those to whom you are obligated to pray; remember also in your petitions the Souls in Purgatory.
Let this entire offering be made in commemoration of and in union with the offering made by Christ on Calvary's hill, when bleeding on the Cross, He offered Himself to His Eternal Father.
Similarly, you may offer for the same intention, the sacrifice of the Mass, wherever it may be celebrated that day throughout the Christian world.

LVI: Concerning Spiritual Communion

Although actual reception of the Sacrament of the Eucharist is limited to once a day, you are nevertheless at liberty to communicate in spirit every hour. And nothing except your own negligence can prevent you from receiving the inestimable benefits to be derived from such a union with Him. It is worth noting that spiritual Communion is sometimes of greater benefit to the soul and more acceptable to God than many sacramental Communions received with little preparation and less affection.

When, therefore, you are properly disposed to receive the Son of God spiritually, be assured that He is ready thus to come to you as food and nourishment.

By way of preparation, think of Jesus, and after contemplating the multitude of your offenses, declare to Him your sincere sorrow for them. Then, with profound respect and unshaking faith, beg Him to condescend graciously to enter your heart; entreat Him to replenish it with grace as a remedy against its inherent weaknesses, and as a shield against the violence of its enemies. Every time you succeed in mortifying your passions, or in performing an act of virtue, take that opportunity of preparing your heart for the Son of God, as He has commanded. Then, addressing yourself to Him, fervently beg the blessings of His presence, both as the physician of your soul and as its protector. Ask Him ever to dwell within your soul and so to take possession of it as to repel its would-be destroyers.

Recall too, your last sacramental communion, and inflamed with love for your Savior, say to Him: "When, O God, shall I receive Thee again? When will that happy day return, when once again you will dwell within my heart?"

If, however, you desire to communicate spiritually with an increase of devotion, begin to prepare for it overnight. Let every mortification and every act of virtue tend to make your soul a more fitting abode for His spiritual presence.

In the morning, as you awake, meditate upon the innumerable advantages to be derived from Holy Communion. Recall that the soul regains her lost virtues, recovers her pristine purity, and is rendered worthy to partake of the merits of the Cross. The very reception of the Sacrament is highly pleasing to the Eternal Father, Who desires everyone to enjoy this Divine gift.

Later endeavor to excite within your soul an ardent desire of receiving Him in compliance with His holy will. Let your words match the sentiment as follows:

"O Lord, since I am not permitted the joy of Thy sacramental presence this day, let Thy goodness and omnipotence decree the cleansing of my soul from the stain of sin, that healed of my wounds, I may deserve to receive Thee in spirit. Every day and every hour, fortified anew by Thy grace, may I courageously resist my enemies, particularly that failing against which for the love of Thee, I wage unceasing war."

LVII: Concerning Thanksgiving

Since all the good we have, or all the good we do, is of God and from God, we are bound in justice to render Him thanks for every good action done, or every victory won in the battle against self. And what is more, we are obliged to render thanks for all blessings, general or particular, which we have received from His bounteous hand.

To do this in a becoming manner, let us consider the end because of which He has heaped upon us the abundance of His blessings; for from such considerations we come to learn how God would be thanked. And as His principal design in all His beneficence is primarily His own honor and the dedication of souls to His Divine service, let everyone reflect within his hearts: "What power, wisdom and goodness has God displayed in bestowing this grace and blessing upon me!" Then considering the incapacity of finite man to merit unaided an infinite favor or even man's utter ingratitude which makes him unworthy of such a blessing we should say in deep humility:

"Is it possible, O Lord, that Thou shouldst love sinful man, the most abject of creatures? How boundless is a love which grants a multitude of blessings to him who deserves it so little! May Thy holy name be blessed now and forever!"

And finally, as such a multitude of blessings requires no more acknowledgment from man than that he love his gracious benefactor, let him thank and love God from the bottom of his heart, resolving to obey completely the dictates of God's holy will. The concluding step consists in the entire offering of self to God, as suggested in the following chapter.

LVIII: The Offering of self to God

There are two things necessary to make our self-oblation completely acceptable to God. One is that it be made in union with the offering made by Christ to the Father; and the other is that it be totally free from all attachment to creatures.

1. As regards the first, we must remember that the Son of God, during His sojourn on earth, offered to His heavenly Father, not only Himself and His works, but also us and our works. Thus must our oblation be made in union with His, and dependent upon His, that both may be sanctified in the sight of the Almighty.

2. With regard to the second, we must remember that we can hardly offer ourselves to Heaven, if we are bound to earth by worldly attachments. Therefore, if we perceive ourselves to be bound by the slightest earthly affection, let us have recourse to God, imploring Him to break asunder the bonds which chain us to earth that we may be His alone. This is of great importance. For if he who is a slave to creatures, pretends to give himself to God while bound to creatures, he gives what is not his, for he is the property of those creatures to whom he has given his will. To offer to God what has been given to crea-

tures is to mock the Almighty. Thus it is that although we have offered ourselves as a holocaust to the Lord, yet we have not only failed to advance in the way of virtue, but have even contracted fresh imperfections, and increased the number of our sins.

We may indeed offer ourselves to God while still attached to creatures, but it must be with the hope that His goodness will set us free, and that we may consecrate ourselves entirely to His service. Therefore let all our offerings be pure and untainted, destined to the honor of God alone. Let us be oblivious of the good things of both Heaven and earth, having nothing in mind but the accomplishment of the will of God, and adoring His Divine Providence. Let us sacrifice every affection of our souls to Him and, forgetting earthly things, let us say:

"Behold, O my God and Creator, the offering I make of my entire being I submit my will entirely to thine; dispose of me as Thou wouldst in life and in death, in time or eternity."

If we make this prayer from the depths of our hearts, our sincerity will be tested in time of adversity, and we shall prove ourselves to be citizens of Heaven, not of earth. We shall be children of God and He will be ours; for He dwells constantly with those who, renouncing themselves and all other creatures, offer themselves up as holocausts to His Divine Majesty.

Here, then, you find a powerful means of vanquishing your enemies; for if, in uniting yourself to God, you become all His, and He all yours, what power or what enemy can ever harm you? And when you would offer fasting, prayers, acts of patience, or good deeds, think first of the oblation of works, prayers, and fasts offered by Christ to His Father, and place all confidence in their infinite merit. But if we desire to offer to this Father of Mercy the sufferings of His son in satisfaction for our sins, we may do so in the following manner:

First, we must call to mind, either in general or particular, the chief disorders of our past lives; and convinced of our inadequacy to appease the Divine wrath of our sovereign Judge, or satisfy His o ended justice, we must have recourse to the life and passion of our Savior. We must remember that when He prayed, fasted, labored, and shed His Precious Blood, He offered all His acts and sufferings to reconcile us with His Almighty Father, saying, as it were: "Behold, O Eternal Father, according to Thy will, how I comply with Thy decrees in atoning for the sins of N. May it please Thy Divine Majesty to grant pardon to him and graciously to receive him into the number of Thy elect."

Everyone ought to join his prayers with those of Jesus Christ, and implore the Eternal Father to have mercy on him through the merits of the Passion and death of His Son. This may be done every time we meditate on the life or Passion of Our Lord, not only in considering the individual mysteries, but also the various circumstances of each of the mysteries. The mode of oblation may apply whether our prayers be offered up for self or for others.

Final Remarks on Prayer and the Combat

LIX: Concerning Sensible Devotion and Dryness

Sensible devotion is sometimes produced by dispositions of our nature, sometimes by artifices of the devil, and sometimes by an influx of grace. You may discern its origin in a particular case by studying the effects; for if no amendment follows, you may well suspect the devil or your own infirm nature to be at the bottom of such devotion, particularly if it be accompanied by much consolation, complacency, or by any measure of self- esteem.

When, therefore, your heart rejoices in exultation and spiritual delight, be not over solicitous to trace their origins; but at the same time, attribute no particular significance to them, and be- ware of inflating your opinion of self. Rather, be ever mindful of your own nothingness, and breaking asunder the fetters of earthly attachments and even spiritual attractions attach yourself to God alone, seeking always to obey the least dictate of His Divine will. This method of conduct will change the very nature of the consolation you experience, and although it should first arise from a defective source, it will later prove most beneficial.

Dryness, or spiritual aridity, proceeds from the following causes:

❖ From the Devil, who strives with satanic vigor to make us become negligent, to lead us from the path of perfection, and plunge us anew into the vanities of the world.

❖ From ourselves, through our own faults, negligences and earthly attachments.

❖ From the Divine grace infused into our souls by the Holy Spirit, not only to wean us away from all that is not of God or tending to Him, but also that we may learn from experience that all things come from Him. Other reasons for such spiritual aridity are: to teach us to esteem His gifts more highly in the future, and show more humility and care in preserving them, and to unite us more closely to His Divine Majesty by an entire renunciation of self, complete to the exclusion of spiritual comforts. For if our affections are centered on spiritual consolation, that heart which Our Lord would keep wholly for Himself is divided.

The last reason to be assigned for such dryness may be the joy God derives from seeing us fight with all our strength, utilizing all His grace to best effect.

When, therefore, you find yourself oppressed with dryness and distaste for spiritual things, ascertain whether or not it is to be attributed to any fault of your own, and if so, amend it instantly, not so much with a view to regaining that sensible enjoyment, but in order to banish everything that is the least displeasing to God. If, however, after careful scrutiny, you can discover no such fault, be not concerned about recovering your sensible fervor; rather exert yourself in the acquisition of that perfect devotion which consists in perfect conformity to the will of God. However barren and insipid your usual exercises may seem, be resolute and persevering in your execution of them, drinking cheerfully the bitter cup the heavenly Father has presented to you.

And if, besides this dryness which makes you almost insensible to heavenly things, you labor under an oppressive cloud of spiritual darkness which makes you fearful, and ignorant of which way to turn, be not discouraged. Let nothing separate you from the Cross of Christ, and disdain all human consolation, vain and wretched as it is.

Be careful, moreover, not to divulge this affliction to anyone but your spiritual director, to whom it should be revealed not with a view to any alleviation, but in order to learn how to bear it in perfect resignation to the Divine will. Offer not your Communions, prayers, or other devout exercises that you may be free of your cross, but that you may receive strength to exalt that cross forever to the honor and glory of Jesus crucified.

And if, from confusion of mind, you can neither pray nor meditate as usual, yet you must persist in those exercises with as little anxiety as possible, supplying for the defects of the mind the affection of the will. Employ vocal prayer, conversing both with yourself and your Savior. Such a practice will have surprising effects, and it will afford you great consolation in your anxiety. On such occasions say to yourself:

> *"Quare tristis es, anima mea, et quare conturbas me? Spera in Deo, quoniam adhuc con te- bor illi, salutare vultus mei et Deus meus . . . Ut quid Domine, recessisti longe, despicis in opportunitate, in tribulatione? Non me derelinquas usquequaque."* [From Psalm 42]

Call to mind the pious sentiments with which God inspired Sara, the wife of Tobias, in her affliction, and say with her in spirit and in word:

> "My God, all who serve Thee know that if they are visited with trials of affliction in this life, they will be rewarded; if oppressed with affliction they shall be delivered: if punished by Thy justice, they hope in mercy. For Thou delightest not in seeing us perish; Thou sendest a calm after storms, and joy after mourning. O God of Israel, be Thy name forever blessed." (Tobit III)

Remember also thy Christ in the garden and on the Cross abandoned by Him Whose Only beloved Son He was; carry your cross with Him and say from the bottom of your heart:

"Not my will but Thine be done."

Thus by uniting patience with prayer in the voluntary immolation of self to God, you will become truly devout. For, as I have said, true devotion consists in an eager and unswerving will to follow Christ, and to bear the cross at whatever time, in whatever way He shall decide; and it consists too in loving God because He is worthy of our love, and even in forfeiting the sweetness of God for the sake of God.

If the multitudes of those who profess piety would measure advancement in the spiritual life by this true standard, rather than by the saccharine effervescences of a purely sensible devotion, they would be deceived neither by the devil nor by themselves; nor would they be so abominably ungrateful as to murmur against their Lord, and unjustly complain of the gift He bestows upon them. For such situations in which the virtue of patience may be developed and strengthened are truly gifts. On the contrary, these multitudes would exert themselves in serving Him with greater fidelity than ever, being convinced that He permits everything for the greater advancement of His glory and our salvation.

There is another dangerous illusion to which women especially are frequently subject, detesting vice as they do and being sedulously watchful in avoiding occasions of sin. At times, as they are molested by impure and frightful thoughts and even loathsome visions, they become despondent, thinking that God has forsaken them. They cannot conceive of the Holy Spirit dwelling in a soul filled with impure thoughts, and imagine themselves inevitably banished from the divine presence.

Being thus disheartened, they are ready to despair, and half-conquered by the temptation, they think of forsaking their exercises of devotion entirely and returning to Egypt. Blind as they are, they do not see God's goodness in permitting them to be tempted as a preventive measure against human negligence, and also a coercive measure designed to bring prodigal man to closer union with his loving Father. Actually, therefore, it is most thoughtless for them to complain of that which should occasion their unceasing gratitude.

On such occasions, we should consider well the perverse propensities of our wounded nature. For God, Who knows best what is to our ultimate advantage, would make us aware that of ourselves we tend to nothing but sin, and when unaided by Him, fall into innumerable miseries.

After this, we must cultivate within ourselves a loving confidence in His Divine mercy, realizing that since He has been pleased to open our eyes to our danger, He also wishes to free us from it and join us to Him in prayer and confidence; for this we owe Him our most humble thanks.

To advert again to those vile thoughts which are involuntary; it is certain that they are put to flight much sooner by a patient resignation to the anxiety they occasion, and a speedy application of the mind to something else, than by a tumultuous and overanxious resistance.

LX: Concerning the Examination of Conscience

In the examination of conscience, consider three things:
1. The faults committed on the particular day.
2. The occasions of these faults.
3. Your need of alacrity in amending those faults and acquiring the contrary virtues.

With regard to the faults committed each day, recall the recommendations of Chapter Twenty-Six (XXVI), which treats of the mode of behavior to be adopted by one who has fallen into sin. It goes without saying that you must strive with the greatest caution and circumspection to avoid the occasions of these faults. And as to the amendment of these faults and the acquisition of the requisite virtues, you must fortify your will by a firm confidence in God, Who will aid you in remedying the evil habits.

If, however, you find that you have triumphed in the struggle over self or excelled in the performance of a good work, beware of vainglory. Even the memory of such victories should not be too much in your thoughts, lest presumption and vanity steal quietly and insidiously into your heart. Leave, therefore, your good works, whatever they may be, to the mercy of God and, forgetting the triumphs of the past, fortify yourself for the struggles of the future.

As to your thanksgiving for the gifts and favors which the Lord has bestowed upon you in the course of the day, humbly acknowledge Him to be the author of all good, and your protector against myriad unseen foes. Thank Him for having inspired you with good thoughts and for having given you the opportunities of practicing virtue. And finally, thank Him for all His unknown gifts of which you will never know.

LXI: Concerning the Manner in which we are to Persevere in the Spiritual Combat until Death

One of the requirements in the spiritual combat is perseverance in the continual mortification of our unruly passions; for never in this life are they utterly subdued, but take root in the human heart like weeds in fertile soil. This is a battle from which we cannot escape; ours is a foe we cannot evade. The fight against passion will last a lifetime, and he who lays down his arms will be slain.

Moreover, we must combat enemies who hate us with unquenchable fury, and are consecrated to our destruction. The more we would make friends of them, the more they would make derelicts of us.

But be not daunted by their strength or number, for in this war, he alone is conquered who voluntarily surrenders, and the entire power of our enemies is in the hands of that captain under whose banner we fight. And not only will He preserve us from treachery, but He will be our champion. He who is infinitely superior to all the foe will crown you with conquest provided that you, as a warrior, rely not on your own finite powers, but on His almighty power and infinite goodness.

If, however, He seems slow in coming to your aid and apparently leaves you in the withering re of the enemy, be not discouraged; rather fight resolutely in the firm belief that He will convert all things which befall you to your eventual benefit, and even the unexpected crown of victory will be yours.

For your part, never desert your commanding officer, who, for your sake, did not shrink from death itself, and in dying on Calvary's hill, conquered the entire world. Fight courageously under His colors, and lay not down your arms while there is one foe left. For if a single vice is neglected it will be a beam in your eye, and a thorn in your side, constantly hindering you from triumph in your glorious and victorious cause.

At Death

LXII: Concerning Our Preparation against the Enemies who assail us at the Hour of Death

Although our entire life on earth is a continual warfare, it is certain that the last day of battle will be the most dangerous; for he who falls on this day, falls never to rise again.

In order, therefore, to be prepared, we must prepare ourselves now; for he who fights well through life will with greater facility emerge victorious in the final assault. Meditate too on death, considering its significance, for such consideration will remove the terror that strikes when death is nigh, and give your mind greater freedom for the combat.

Worldly men cannot stand the thought of death; they refuse to think of it lest they be distracted from the earthly pleasures in which they have placed their affection. The thought of losing transient things is naturally repugnant and painful to one who is oblivious to eternal things. Thus the affections of worldlings are more firmly riveted to this world day by day. And day by day the contemplation of the loss of worldly things strikes increased terror most frequently into the hearts of those who have enjoyed worldliness the longest.

In order to be prepared for the awesome step from time into eternity, imagine yourself sometime all alone in the face of the agonies of death, and consider the things that would most likely trouble you at that hour. Then imprint deeply in your heart the remedies I shall propose to be employed when the situation is at hand. The blow that can be struck but once should be well rehearsed, as a final error means an eternity of regret and misery.

LXIII: Concerning the four assaults of the Enemy at the Hour of Death: The first assault against Faith and the manner of resisting it.

There are four principal assaults to which the enemy is likely to resort when we are at the threshold of death. They are temptations against faith and to despair, thoughts of vainglory, and finally, various illusions employed by the children of darkness, who are disguised as angels of light.

As to the first assault, depend rather on the will than on the understanding, saying: "Get thee behind me, Satan, father of lies, for I will not even hear thee; it is enough for me to believe as the Holy Catholic Church believes."

Similarly, be sedulously watchful against any thoughts which may appear to be conducive to the strengthening of your faith; reject them instantly as suggestions of the devil, who seeks desperately to lure you into dispute. If, however, you find it impossible to turn your thoughts resolutely from such matters, at least be adamant in your refusal to listen to Scriptural quotations the adversary may glibly present; for although they are apparently clear and precise, they will be invariably garbled, misinterpreted, or incorrectly applied.

If, at this time, the evil one asks what the Church believes, ignore him; but seeing his aim is to surprise or entrap you in words, be content with making a general act of faith. If you wish to mortify him further, answer that the Church believes the truth; and if he wishes to know what truth is, tell him it is what the Church believes and teaches.

Above all, keep your heart intently fixed on Jesus crucified, saying: "My God, My Creator and Redeemer, hurry to my assistance, and stay with me lest I wander from the truth which

Thou hast taught me. Grant that as I was born in the faith, so may I die in the faith to Thy glory and my salvation!"

LXIV: The second assault of Despair and its Remedy

The second assault by which the perverse one attempts our destruction is the terror which he would infuse into our minds at the recollection of our past sins, hoping thereby to drive us to despair.

In this peril, hold fast to the infallible rule that the remembrance of your sins is the effect of grace, and is most salutary if it inspires within your heart sentiments of humility, compunction, and confidence in God's mercy. But if such recollection creates vexation and despondency, leaving you spiritless from the apparent cogency of the reasons adduced to convince you that you are irrevocably lost, be assured that it has been suggested by the devil. In such circumstances, humble yourself the more, and have greater confidence in God; thus shall you destroy the stratagem of the devil, turn his own weapons against him, and give greater glory to God.

It is true that you should be truly contrite for having o ended such sovereign goodness, as often as you call to mind your past offenses; but as often as you ask pardon you should have a firm confidence in the infinite mercy of Jesus Christ.

I will go further and say that even though God Himself should seem to say within your heart that you are not one of His flock, still place your confidence in Him; rather say to Him in all humility: "Thou hast good reason indeed, O Lord, to condemn me for my sins, but I have greater reason in Thy mercy to hope for pardon. Have pity then, O Lord, on a humble sinner condemned by his own sinfulness, but redeemed by Thy Blood. I commit myself entirely to Thy hands, O my Redeemer; all my hopes are in Thee, trusting that in Thine infinite compassion, Thou will save me to the glory of Thy name. Do with me as Thou wilt, for Thou alone art my Lord. Even though, My Lord, Thou shouldst destroy me, ever will I hope in Thee."

LXV: The third assault of Temptation to Vainglory

The third assault is that of vainglory and presumption. Dread nothing so much as yielding in the least way to an exalted opinion of your person or your good works. Take no glory but in the Lord, and acknowledge that all that you are or ever hope to be is to be attributed to the merits of the life and death of Jesus Christ. Until the very evensong of life, hear nothing within your heart but the refrain of your own nothingness. Let your humility deepen as self-love fades, and unceasingly thank God, the Author of all your greatness. Stand ever in a holy and prudent fear, and acknowledge simply that all your endeavors are vain, unless God, in Whom is all your hope, crowns them with success.

If you will follow this advice, never shall your enemy prevail against you; your road will be open before you, and you may pass on joyfully to the heavenly Jerusalem.

LXVI: The fourth assault of various illusions employed by the Devil at the Hour of Death

If our persistent foe, who never ceases to persecute us, should assail us disguised as an angel of light, stand firm and steadfast even though cognizant of your own nothingness, and say to him boldly: "Return, miserable one into your realms of darkness; for I am unworthy of visions, nor do I need anything but the mercy of my Savior, and the prayers of Mary, Joseph and all the Saints."

And though these visions seem to bear many evidences of having been born in Heaven, still reject them as far as it is within your power to do so. And have no fear that this resistance, founded as it is on your own worthiness, will be displeasing to God. For if the vision be from Him, He has the power to make the same known to you, and you will suffer no detriment; for He Who gives grace to the humble does not withdraw it because of acts which spring from humility.

These, then, are the weapons which the enemy most commonly employs against us at the hour of our death. Each individual is tempted according to the particular inclination to which he is most subject. Therefore, before the zero hour of the great conflict, we should arm ourselves securely, and struggle manfully against our most violent passions, that the victory may be easier in that hour which leaves no future time for preparation or resistance.

Treatise on Peace of Soul and Inner Happiness

Of the Soul Which Dies to Self in Order to Live for God

I: The nature of the human heart and the way in which it should be governed

God created the heart of man for no other end than to love Him, and to be loved by Him; and the sublimity of this divine design should convince us that it is the noblest of the works of His almighty hand. Our first obligation, then, is to direct that heart to place its affection in proper things, that exterior acts might flow from interior dispositions of the heart. For although corporal penances and various chastisements of the flesh are praiseworthy when practiced in prudent moderation, yet by this means alone rather than acquiring a single virtue, you will probably acquire conceit and vanity. All externals will prove ineffectual unless they be invigorated by and permeated with worthy internal dispositions.

The life of man is nothing but a continual warfare and temptation; and because it is a warfare, you must watch over your heart with sedulous care that it may be ever at peace. If any movements signal sensual disturbances, take heed to calm the storms within your heart instantly, never permitting the pursuit of vain and illusory pleasures. Exercise this caution not only in time of prayer, but anytime disquieting thoughts assail you, for prayers will be indifferently said until the soul knows peace.

Observe, however, that all this must be done with a certain mildness and effortless ease, as the principal e ort of our lives should be the quieting of our hearts, and the prudent guidance of those hearts lest they go astray.

II: The care to be exercised by the soul in the acquisition of perfect tranquility

The mild, peaceful, constant attention to the feelings of the heart will produce wonderful results; for we shall not only pray and act with great facility and peace, but shall even suffer with-out lamenting the disturbing elements of contempt and the injuries themselves.

It is necessary, however, to undergo much toil before we acquire this serenity, for our inexperience inevitably exposes us to the assaults of powerful enemies. But once acquired, this peace will bring untold consolation to our souls in their fight against the disquieting elements of the world, and daily we shall perfect the art of quieting the turmoil of the spirit.

If at times you are in such confusion of mind that you seem totally incapable of calming yourself, have immediate recourse to prayer. And persevere in it in imitation of Christ, Our Lord, Who prayed three times in the garden to show mankind that only in conversation with God can afflicted souls find haven and refuge.

Let us pray without ceasing that repose may replace the chaos in our hearts, and that a humble submissiveness to God's will may bring our soul to its former tranquility.

Let us not be disturbed by the endless and pointless hurry of the business world; when we are at work, let us attend to business a airs with composure and ease, refraining from rigid conformity to a harsh, exacting schedule, and too great an eagerness to see our work done

Our principal intention, a continual awareness of God's holy presence, and an unchanging desire to please Him, should preside over all our actions. And if we permit any other consideration to interfere, our souls will soon abound with fear and anxiety; we shall often fall, and the difficulty of recovering will convince us that our evils proceed invariably from acting in compliance with our own will and inclination. If on such occasions we are successful, then we are puffed up with vain satisfaction; and if we are disappointed, we are overwhelmed by uneasiness and vexation.

III: The necessity of building this peaceful habitation by degrees

B anish from your mind whatever tends to depress and disconcert you, striving always with great mildness to acquire or preserve serenity of soul. For Christ Himself has said: "Blessed are the peacemakers. . . . Learn of me for I am meek and humble of heart." Never doubt that God will crown your labor and make your soul a dwelling of delight; all He asks of you is a sincere attempt to disperse the clouds and storms whenever you are molested by disturbances of the senses and passions, that the sun of peace may shine on all your actions.

As a house cannot be built in a day, neither can the mansion of inner peace be built within our souls in a fleeting instant. Rather, our success is a gradual attainment; it is the culmination of the primary work of the divine architect in predisposing our souls for the edifice to be built therein, and the firm establishment of humility which must be the foundation of that edifice.

IV: The necessity of relinquishing human consolations in the acquisition of inner peace

The path which leads to this heavenly peace is almost unknown to the world. For along that path tribulations and trials are sought with the same avidity that the worldling displays in the pursuit of pleasure. There contempt and derision are pursued as are honors and glory by the ambitious; there as great pains are taken to neglect and be neglected, to forsake and be forsaken, as the children of this world take to be sought for, caressed, and admired by the mighty and the rich. And there holy ambition is known, comforted, and favored by God alone.

The Christian soul, as it travels this path, learns to converse with God alone and to be so strongly fortified by His presence, that it is willing to suffer anything for Him and the promotion of His glory.

There one learns that suffering blots out the sun, and that affliction endured in the proper manner is a treasure laid up for eternity; and there one learns too that to suffer with Jesus Christ is the only ambition of the soul which seeks the glory of resembling Him.

There one is taught that to love ourselves, to follow our own wills, to obey our sensual appetites, and to destroy ourselves are one and the same thing. There one is taught too that our own will is not even to be gratified in what is commendable, until we have submitted it in all simplicity and humility of heart to the will of God; that what He ordains and not what we wish should be the rule of our actions.

Frequently we perform good works from wrong motives, or through indiscreet zeal, which, like the false prophet, appears to be an innocent lamb, when in reality it is a ravenous wolf. The devout soul, however, will discover the illusion from the effects produced. When it finds itself in trouble and anxiety, humility diminished and composure disturbed; when it no longer enjoys peace and tranquility, and perceives all that has been attained with much time and labor to be lost then the fact is really fantasy.

We may sometimes fall on the path to inner peace; but this only serves to increase humility which assists us to recover and to watch more strictly over ourselves in the future. Perhaps God permits us to fall in order to root out some secret fault, artfully concealed by our deceitful self-love.

Sometimes, too, the soul may be molested with temptations to sin, but it must not be unduly disturbed on this account; rather must the soul quietly withdraw from such temptations, reinstating itself in its former tranquility without indulging in an excess of either joy or sorrow.

In a word, all we must do is to keep our souls in purity and peace in the sight of God, knowing by experience that He ordains everything for our ultimate welfare.

V: The necessity of keeping the soul disengaged and in solitude that God's Holy Will may operate in it

If we are truly cognizant of the priceless worth of the immortal soul, that sublime temple of God Himself, let us take care that nothing of the world intrude therein. Placing our hope in the Lord, we should wait with a firm confidence for His coming, and realize that He will certainly enter the soul unattached to worldly things and ready to receive Him alone. Alone, having no desire but the presence of God; alone, loving only Him; alone, void of all will but the will of Heaven.

Let us learn to do nothing to please ourselves, that we may merit in the soul of the human the presence of the Divine, the comprehension of Whom is far beyond the horizons of created intellects.

Let us follow exactly the prescriptions of our spiritual father and of those who govern us in the place of God, that every suffering and good work offered to God may be prudent and salutary.

It is sufficient that we keep ourselves ever ready and willing to suffer for love of Him all that He wills and the manner in which He wills it. Whoever acts solely in conjunction with the dictates of his own will would do much better were he to remain in peace, attentive to what God wills to perform in him. Therefore, we must always avoid attachments of the will which should ever be free and in perfect harmony with the Divine.

And since we ought not to act according to our desires, let

us not consciously attach our wills to anyone thing; but if we should desire something, let it be in such a way as to leave us as unperturbed as if we had desired nothing, should our desire fail to materialize.

Our desires are our chains, and to be entangled in them is to be a slave. To free ourselves from desires, therefore, is to free ourselves from tyranny.

God demands that our souls be alone and unattached that He may manifest His manifold wonders in them, glorifying them even in this life by His Divine power.

O Holy Solitude! O desert of happiness! O glorious hermitage, where a soul may find its God! Let us not only run to such an exalted place, but beg the wings of a dove that we may fly to it and find there a holy repose. Let us not stop by the wayside; let us not tarry on the way for frivolous conversation; let us leave the dead to bury their dead, forsaking the land of the lifeless for the land of the living.

VI: The necessity of our love of neighbor being guided by prudence that serenity of soul be not disturbed

God does not dwell in a soul which He does not first inflame with a love of Him and charity for others; for Christ Himself said He came to set the world on re.

Although our love of God must have no bounds, our charity for our neighbor must have its limits. We cannot love our God too much, but if our love for others is not guided by prudent moderation, we may destroy ourselves in seeking to save others.

Let us, therefore, love our neighbor in a manner which will not be deleterious to our own souls; this is best accomplished by doing nothing with the sole aim of setting them a good example, lest in saving them we lose ourselves. Rather our actions should be performed with great simplicity and sanctity, with the sole aim of pleasing God in humble acknowledgment of the limited value of our good works to ourselves and others. We are not expected to be so zealous for the salvation of others, as to destroy the peace of our own souls.

We may ardently desire their illumination when God is pleased that we do so; but we must not wait for a Divine communication nor vainly imagine that it is to be acquired by our exaggerated solicitude and imprudent zeal.

Let us seek the peace and repose of a holy solitude, for such is the will of God as it binds us closer to Him; and let us remain recollected and undisturbed until the lord of the vineyard requires our services. God will clothe us with Himself when He finds us divested of all earthly care and solicitude.

When we have forgotten ourselves, God will not forget us; peace will reign in our hearts, and Divine love will grant us an undisturbed facility of action, as well as moderation and temperance in all that we do. Thus every action of our lives shall be performed in the repose of a Heaven-sent peace in which even silence is eloquent; and to be free of earthly care in order to offer ourselves to the service of the Master is to act in accordance with the will of Christ. For it is His Divine goodness that must work in us and with us, requiring no more of us than sufficient humility to present to Him a soul that has but one desire, and this desire is that God's will be accomplished in us in the most perfect possible manner.

VII: The necessity of divesting our souls entirely of their own will, that they may be presented to God

"Come to me all ye that labor and are burdened, and I will refresh you . . . all you that thirst, come to the fountain." Such are the words of Christ in the Scriptures; let us follow this Divine summons, without impulsiveness or clamor, in peace and mildness, referring ourselves respectfully and confidently to our loving and omnipotent God.

Let us wait calmly for the coming of that spirit which

brings peace; let us, entirely resigned and obedient to the decrees of His holy will, think of nothing but the means by which He may be desired, loved and glorified.

Let these acts be performed without using force or violence on our hearts, lest by an unwise use of these instruments, our souls be rendered incapable of that sweet repose, which on this earth is their glory.

Rather let us gradually accustom our souls to contemplate nothing but the love and goodness of God; let them be ever mindful of the Heavenly manna with which they shall be nourished in ineffable sweetness, once they accustom themselves to frequent meditation on these sublime truths. Avoid shedding useless tears or striving to excite within yourself an emotional display of devotion; but abide quietly in interior solitude until the will of God is accomplished in you. And when He gives you tears, they shall be sweet and effortless; accept them with gentleness and serenity, and above all with humility. By these indications shall you ascertain the source from which they spring, receiving them as dew from Heaven itself.

Let us not presume to know, have, or desire particular things, for the very cornerstone of the spiritual edifice is not dependent on our knowledge, possessions, or desires in the slightest degree. Rather should we remain in a state of perfect self-denial like Mary at the feet of Jesus, instead of busying ourselves with many things like Martha.

When you seek God by the light of your human understanding, you must avoid purely human concepts, or comparisons which limit, or inadvertently circumscribe His unbounded greatness. For He is beyond all comparison; He is beyond all division, He is omnipresent, containing all things in Himself.

Try to visualize a limitless immensity, a unity which really defies human comprehension, and a power which has created and sustains all things in the entire universe in a feat of inimitable grandeur. Then say humbly within your soul: "Behold thy God."

Contemplate and admire Him unceasingly in all times and in all places, for as He is everywhere, He is in your soul, and in it He rejoices as He has said. And although the Almighty stands in not the slightest need of your soul, He is pleased to make it a worthy habitation of Himself.

In your intellectual pursuit of these sublime truths, be sure to retain a calm and peaceful will. Strive not to limit yourself to so many prayers, meditations, or readings, neither neglect nor limit your customary devotions. Rather let your heart be at liberty to stop where it finds its God, having no misgivings about unfinished exercises if He is pleased to communicate Himself to you in the midst of them. Have no scruples in this regard, for the end of your devotion is to enjoy God, and as the end is accomplished, the means have no significance for the present.

God leads us by the path that He has chosen, and if we oblige ourselves to precise execution of exercises which we fancy, we are imposing imaginary obligations on ourselves; and far from finding God, we are actually running away from Him, pretending to please Him, yet not conforming to His holy will.

If you really desire to advance successfully on this path, and attain the end to which it leads, seek and desire God alone; and whenever and wherever you find Him, there stop, go no farther. While God dwells with you enjoy His company with the celestial peace of Saints; and when His Divine majesty pleases to retire, then turn again to the quest of your God in your devout exercises.

This advice is of the greatest importance and well merits our attention. For frequently we see many clerics who exhaust themselves in the fatiguing execution of their duties without deriving any advantages for themselves, or finding peace. For they imagine they have done nothing if they leave their task unfinished, believing perfection to consist in constant adherence to the minutest prescriptions of their own wills. Thus their lives are spent in weariness and toil as one who labors fruitlessly through the years; never do they obtain that true repose and interior peace in which the Lord truly dwells, for it is the peaceful soul that is a sanctuary of Jesus Christ.

VIII: Concerning our faith in the Blessed Sacrament, and the method by which we are to offer ourselves to God

OUR FAITH and love in the Holy Eucharist must so increase and strengthen as to become almost part of the very fiber of our being. Such faith and love cannot be successfully cultivated without a disciplined will, prepared to undergo all afflictions, tribulations, infirmities, and spiritual dryness for the sake of Jesus Christ. It is not for us to ask Him to change Himself into us, rather should we humbly petition to be changed into Him.

Entertain Him not with pompous speeches or empty words. Admiration and exultation should so engulf our souls as to sub- merge these functions, as it were, when He is present. Our understanding should be completely absorbed in joyous contemplation of this incomprehensible mystery, and our heart suffused with joy at the sight of such immense majesty under such simple appearances. And let us desire no further manifestation of His divinity, remembering His deathless words: "Blessed are they who have not seen, and have believed."

Above all let us be constant and punctual in our devotions, and practice unceasingly those means most conducive to purifying and adorning our souls with a peaceful and mild simplicity. And while these methods are followed, the grace of perseverance will never be wanting to us.

A soul which has once known the ineffable delight of spiritual peace can never return to the hurry and confusion of a worldly life; for it is impossible for her to endure it in such circumstances.

IX: True happiness is not to be found in pleasure or comfort, but in God alone

A soul which is deliberately oblivious of the goods of this world, but relishes its mortifications and persecutions, which neither loves all it can bestow nor dreads all it can inflict, which avoids honors as it would a contagion, and cherishes humiliation as a beloved thing such a soul may expect all consolation from God, provided it relies on the strength of God rather than on the weakness of self.

The courage of St. Peter was very great when he declared his resolution of dying with Christ, and his will apparently strong enough to merit commendation, but in reality Peter's reliance was a reliance on his own will, and this was the occasion of his shameful fall. How true it is that we can neither propose nor execute good, unless supported by the almighty power of God.

Let us purge our soul of all desires that nothing may impede its operations in the particular situation. This is not to say that one must ignore temporal a airs entirely, for they are to be man- aged with a prudent and commendable solicitude in accordance with the circumstances of the individual. Such management of temporal a airs is completely in harmony with the Divine will, and is in no way at variance with our inner peace of soul and spiritual advancement.

We can do nothing better towards pro table employment of the particular time than to offer the soul, entirely divested of all desires, to almighty God, standing humbly before Him as a miserable culprit, incapable of doing anything for himself.

In this freedom of mind and disengagement of self in which there is utter dependence on God alone, we find the essence of perfection. And it is impossible to conceive how God loves and blesses those who have unselfishly consecrated themselves to Him completely. He is pleased to receive confidence without reserve, and he delights in enlightening them, in resolving their difficulties, in forgiving the offenses of the truly penitent, and in raising them when fallen.

For God is still the priest forever, and though He has given to St. Peter and his successors the power of loosing and binding, He has not divested Himself of those powers. So if the penitent cannot have recourse to their confessors as often as they wish, the divine majesty receives them in His infinite mercy, pardoning their sins whenever they approach Him with true confidence, perfect sorrow, and entire love. Such are the fruits of this detachment from self.

X: The necessity of not being dejected at the obstacles and repugnance we find in the acquisition of this interior peace

God is often pleased to permit our inner serenity, this solitude and holy peace of soul, to be disturbed and overcast with the clouds and emotions arising from our self-love and natural inclinations. But as His goodness permits these trials for our greater good, He will not fail to bestow the refreshing showers of His Divine consolation on this dryness of spirit, enriching the soul with the fruits and flowers of His undying love.

These interruptions of our tranquility occasioned by the emotions of the sensitive appetites are the very combats in which the saints gained victories which merited them immortal crowns.

Whenever you fall into such weakness, disgust and desolation of spirit, say to God with an humble and affectionate heart: "Lord, I am the work of Thy hands and the slave redeemed by Thy precious blood; dispose of me as entirely Thine, made for Thee alone, and grant that my only hope may be in Thee." Thrice happy is the soul which thus offers itself to God in time of affliction!

Perhaps under particular circumstances you find yourself unable to bend your will immediately to an entire submission to God; if such is the case, you should not be dejected, for it is the cross the Master has commanded you to bear as you follow Him. Did He not first bear the cross of Golgotha to show you how to bear your little cross of earthly affliction? Contemplate His combat in the garden when He struggled with His human nature, the weakness of which made Him cry out: "Father, if it is possible, let this cup pass away from Me." And remember the soul that rose above the weakness of the body, to cry out in profound humility: "Not My will but Thine be done."

Perhaps the weakness of human nature may make you try to avoid all trouble or affliction, and at such times you may show your dislike which prompts you to keep suffering at a distance.

Nevertheless, be sure you persevere in prayer and acts of humility until you find no other desire or inclination than the accomplishment of God's holy will in your soul.

Try to keep your heart reserved for God alone, that there may be no room for bitterness, gall, or voluntary repugnance to what God shall appoint. Never be absorbed in the failings of others, but pursue your own path, regarding nothing but that which may wound your conscience. The great secret of belonging to God is to neglect and pass by everything else.

XI: Concerning the artifices of the devil to destroy our peace of soul, and the method of combating them

The enemy of mankind endeavors chiefly to withdraw us from a state of humility and Christian simplicity by suggesting to us our superiority over others; this is soon followed by our manifestation of a critical attitude, and a contemptuous regard of the failings of others. The greatest means utilized by the evil one in stealing into our souls, however, is our own vanity and self-love; and the art of defeating him is to keep deeply entrenched in holy humility without ever forsaking it. If we do not attempt to so discipline self, we abandon ourselves to the proud spirit for whom we are no match. And once he gets possession of our wills, he plays the tyrant to perfection, introducing every vice into our souls.

It is not sufficient that we watch; we must also pray. For it has been said that we must watch and pray, and peace of mind is a treasure which cannot be secured unless it is thus guarded.

Let us not suffer our minds to be afflicted or disturbed on any account whatever. The humble and peaceful soul does everything with a facility that vaults over obstacles with grace and ease; its conduct is holy and the soul perseveres in it. But the soul which permits itself to be perturbed performs few good actions of any significance, and suffers continually but to no advantage.

You will discern whether thoughts are to be encouraged or banished by the confidence or diffidence they inspire in the Divine mercy. If they suggest the continual increase of affectionate confidence, you are to look upon them as messengers from Heaven, entertaining them and delighting in them. But you are to banish as the suggestion of Hell itself all thoughts that make you the least di dent of His infinite goodness.

The tempter of pious souls often magnifies their imperfections, persuading the faithful that they are unfaithful to their duties, imperfect in Confessions, tepid at Communion, and deficient in prayer. Thus with various scruples he keeps them in constant alarm, seeking to distract them from their exercises, as if God had forgotten or forsaken them. Nothing can be more false than to believe this, for the advantages arising from distractions, spiritual dryness, and the like, are innumerable, provided the soul comprehends and complies with what God expects of her in those circumstances. And God only expects patience and perseverance. For the prayers and exercises of a soul, deprived of all satisfaction in what she does, is the delight of the Almighty, according to St. Gregory.

Particularly is such a soul pleasing to God if, notwithstanding its insensibility and apathy, it persists with courage. For the patience of such a soul is a prayer in itself, prevailing more with God than any prayers said with great emotional fervor. St. Gregory adds that the interior darkness with which such a devotion is surrounded shines brightly in the presence of God, and that nothing we do can sooner draw us to Him or evoke from Him fresh gifts of grace.

Never forsake, therefore, any work of piety, however disinclined religiously you may be, unless you would comply with the wishes of Satan. Learn from the following chapter, innumerable advantages to be reaped through a humble perseverance in works of piety, when attended with the most irksome spiritual barrenness.

XII: The necessity of preserving equanimity of soul in the midst of internal temptations

Spiritual barrenness and aridity bestow innumerable benefits upon the soul if accepted in the proper spirit of humility and patience. The thorough mastery of this secret would indeed pre- vent many uneasy days and unhappy hours of perturbation of spirit.

How utterly mistaken we are in thinking ourselves forsaken and abhorred by God Almighty, and deprived of the treasured tokens of His Divine love; how erroneous to fancy ourselves punished by His anger, when actually we are favored by His goodness. Can we not see that the uneasiness which arises from such interior aridity can only spring from a desire of being altogether acceptable to God and zealous and fervent in His service? Such uneasiness rarely happens at the beginning of one's conversion to the service of God; rather it is found in those who have already consecrated themselves for some time to the Master, and are resolved to travel the paths of perfection.

On the contrary, we seldom hear the inveterate sinner or the worldling complain of such temptations. Thus we may well believe that these trials constitute a precious food by which God nourishes those whom He loves. Even though the temptation is so violent as to strike terror into our hearts, we shall derive innumerable blessings from it; for the blessing derived will be in proportion to the severity of our trial.

Such a situation the soul does not always understand, and shrinks from the path of crosses and afflictions. This is simply to say that the soul is unwilling to be deprived of delight and consolation, and whatever devotion is not accompanied by an emotional glow, so to speak, is erroneously esteemed to be no better than lost labor.

XIII: God permits temptations for our ultimate welfare

We are by nature proud, ambitious, and ever mindful to the whims of our sense appetites. Hence it is that we are apt to flatter ourselves continually, and esteem ourselves out of all proportion to our merit.

Such presumption is so great an obstacle to our spiritual progress, that the slightest taint of it impedes us in the attainment of true perfection. It is an evil which we do not always discern, but God, Who loves us and knows the true viciousness of presumption, is watchful in rescuing us from this deceit, waking us from the lethargy of self-love and bringing us to true self-knowledge.

Did He not once rescue the erring Peter when He permitted that Apostle to deny Him, and forswear any knowledge of his Lord? Did He not grant to Peter self-knowledge and strength to cast aside his dangerous presumption? Did He not similarly deal with St. Paul when, in order to preserve him from this insidious vice and prevent him from making an improper use of the sub- lime revelations entrusted to him, He permitted a troublesome temptation to constantly remind the Apostle of his weakness?

Let us admire, then, the beneficence and wisdom of God, Who so treats us for our own good, favoring us imperceptibly, even when we imagine He is afflicting us.

We are perhaps prone to attribute our tepidity to our imperfections, and our emotional apathy toward the things of God; and we are easily persuaded that no one is so distracted or forsaken as ourselves, that God has no servants as wretched as we are, and that none but miscreants have their minds filled with thoughts like ours.

Thus by the effects of this heavenly medicine is the patient, once swollen with presumption, reduced in his own opinion to the status of an unworthy Christian.

Would such a transformation ever happen were man left to his own devices? Would man himself willingly descend from the lofty pinnacles of pride? Would he have been ever cured of his haughtiness? Would the illusory clouds of vanity have been dispelled from his head and heart without this Divine remedy?

Humility is not the only benefit to be derived from such temptations, afflictions, and interior desolation which leaves the soul weary and disconsolate, depriving it of all emotional sweetness in devotion. For such trials compel us to have recourse to God, to fly from everything displeasing to Him, and to apply ourselves with greater diligence to the practice of virtue. Such afflictions are a kind of Purgatory, which burn away the dross from our souls, and gain us crowns of glory when received with humility and patience.

The soul, convinced of the above truths, may judge whether or not it should be disturbed and grieves at losing a taste for devotional exercises or being engulfed in interior temptations. And it may judge too whether or not it is reasonable to attribute to the devil what comes from God, and to mistake the tokens of His tenderness for marks of His indignation.

On such an occasion all the soul needs do is to humble itself in the sight of God; to persevere and bear with patience the disgust it finds in exercises of devotion; to conform to the Divine will, and try to preserve equanimity of soul by humble acquiescence to His decrees. Such is the will of our Father, Who is in Heaven.

Instead of languishing in sorrow and dejection, the soul should bloom forth into acts of thanksgiving, establishing itself in peace and submission to the appointments of Heaven.

XIV: The mode of behavior to be adopted with regard to our faults

If it should happen that you commit a fault in word or deed, give way to anger, interrupt your devotions out of some vain curiosity, indulge in immoderate joy or frivolity, entertain suspicious thoughts of your neighbor, or succumb to any failing, be not disquieted. Even if you fail often, succumbing to a fault against which you have made firm resolutions, do not permit such failure to depress and afflict you, considering your- self incapable of amendment, and careless in your devotion. For such troublesome thoughts torture the soul and consume much valuable time.

Neither should you dwell too long in sifting the various circumstances of your faults, such as the thoroughness of deliberation or degree of consent; for such considerations only serve to perplex your mind, both before and after Confession, and fill you with uneasiness.

You would not be so much molested with these cares were you well aware of your own inherent weakness, and the conduct you should adopt towards God Almighty after committing such faults. Anxiety and dejection of mind do no good, but only disturb and depress the spirit. By turning to Him, however, with great humility and affection, you are manifesting the proper mode of behavior. And this is to be advocated as regards great faults as well as peccadilloes, not only in those faults occasioned by sloth and tepidity, but even those occasioned by malice itself.

This point is not adequately understood by many; for instead of practicing this great lesson of filial confidence in the goodness and mercy of God, their spirits are so wasted that they are as ineffectual in the execution of a good work as they are in its conception. Thus they lead a miserable, languishing existence, by preferring their own weak imaginations to sound wholesome doctrine in which their welfare consists.

XV: The soul without loss of time should compose itself and make steady progress

As often as you are guilty of any fault, great or small, frequent or rare, you should adopt the following procedure as soon as you are aware of what you have done. Consider your own weakness, and humbly have recourse to God, saying to Him with a calm and loving confidence: "Thou hast seen, O my God, that I did what I could; Thou hast seen my impotence and, as Thou hast given me the grace to repent, I beseech Thee to add to my pardon the grace never to offend Thee again."

Once you have finished this prayer, do not torture yourself with anxious thoughts on your forgiveness, but without further adverting to your fall, proceed in your devotions with humility and ease, seeking the same tranquility and peace of mind as before.

This method is to be observed as often as the fault is repeated though it were a thousand times, with as much sincerity and fervor after the last fault as after the first. For this is the way we return immediately to God, Who, like a tender father, is ready to receive us as often as we come to Him.

Such a practice also prevents loss of time in fruitless anxiety which only ruffles the serenity of the mind, and prevents it from resuming its usual calmness and fidelity.

I ardently wish that those who grow disconsolate upon committing faults would study well this spiritual secret. They would soon understand how different is their state from a humble cheerful mind where peace and tranquility reign. They would soon understand the utter fruitlessness and loss of time caused by anxiety and worry.

About the Editor

Scott Smith is a Catholic author, attorney, and theologian. He and his wife Ashton are the parents of four wild-eyed children and live in their hometown of New Roads, Louisiana.

Check out more of his writing and courses below …

More from Scott Smith

Scott regularly contributes to his blog, The Scott Smith Blog at www.thescottsmithblog.com, WINNER of the 2018-2019 Fisher's Net Award for Best Catholic Blog:

FISHER'S NET AWARD
BEST CATHOLIC
BLOG 2018

— THE —
SCOTT SMITH BLOG
ALL ROADS LEAD TO ROME

AS SEEN ON ...
NATIONAL CATHOLIC
REGISTER
ChurchPOP
Aleteia
BIG PULPIT
New Advent
Catholic Online
SPIRIT DAILY
ALL
SAINTS
UNIVERSITY
CATHOLICISM.ORG

Scott's other books can be found at his publisher's, Holy Water Books, website, holywaterbooks.com, as well as on Amazon

His other books on theology and the Catholic faith include *The Catholic ManBook, Everything You Need to Know About Mary But Were Never Taught,* and *Blessed is He Who ...* (Biographies of Blesseds). More on these below ...

His fiction includes *The Seventh Word,* a pro-life horror novel, and the *Cajun Zombie Chronicles,* the Catholic version of the zombie apocalypse.

ALL
SAINTS
UNIVERSITY
EST. MMXVII

Scott has also produced courses on the Blessed Mother and Scripture for All Saints University.

Learn about the Blessed Mary from anywhere and learn to defend your mother! It includes over six hours of video plus a free copy of the next book ... Enroll Now!

What You *Need* to Know About Mary
But Were Never Taught

Pray the Rosary with St. John Paul II

St. John Paul II said "the Rosary is my favorite prayer." So what could possibly make praying the Rosary even better? Praying the Rosary with St. John Paul II!

This book includes a reflection from John Paul II for every mystery of the Rosary. You will find John Paul II's biblical re-

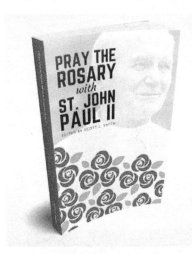

flections on the twenty mysteries of the Rosary that provide practical insights to help you not only understand the twenty mysteries but also live them.

St. John Paul II said "The Rosary is my favorite prayer. A marvelous prayer! Marvelous in its simplicity and its depth. In the prayer we repeat many times the words that the Virgin Mary heard from the Archangel, and from her kinswoman Elizabeth."

St. John Paul II said "the Rosary is the storehouse of countless blessings." In this new book, he will help you dig even deeper into the treasures contained within the Rosary.

You will also learn St. John Paul II's spirituality of the Rosary: "To pray the Rosary is to hand over our burdens to the merciful hearts of Christ and His mother."

"The Rosary, though clearly Marian in character, is at heart a Christ-centered prayer. It has all the depth of the gospel message in its entirety. It is an echo of the prayer of Mary, her perennial Magnificat for the work of the redemptive Incarnation which began in her virginal womb."

Take the Rosary to a whole new level with St. John Paul the Great! St. John Paul II, *pray for us!*

What You Need to Know About Mary But Were Never Taught

Give a robust defense of the Blessed Mother using Scripture. Now, more than ever, every Catholic needs to learn how to defend their mother, the Blessed Mother. Because now, more than ever, the family is under attack and needs its Mother.

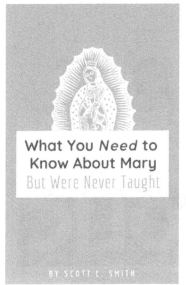

Discover the love story, hidden within the whole of Scripture, of the Father for his daughter, the Holy Spirit for his spouse, and the Son for his MOTHER.

This collection of essays and the All Saints University course made to accompany it will demonstrate through Scripture how the Immaculate Conception of Mary was prophesied in Genesis.

It will also show how the Virgin Mary is the New Eve, the New Ark, and the New Queen of Israel.

Catholic Nerds Podcast

As you might have noticed, Scott is obviously well-credentialed as a nerd. Check out Scott's podcast: the Catholic Nerds Podcast on iTunes, Podbean, Google Play, and wherever good podcasts are found!

The Catholic ManBook

Do you want to reach Catholic Man LEVEL: EXPERT? *The Catholic ManBook* is your handbook to achieving Sainthood, manly Sainthood. Find the following resources inside, plus many others:

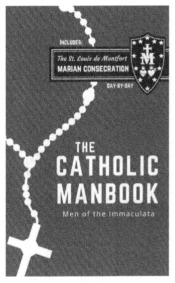

- Top Catholic Apps, Websites, and Blogs
- Everything you need to pray the Rosary
- The Most Effective Daily Prayers & Novenas, including the Emergency Novena
- Going to Confession and Eucharistic Adoration like a boss!
- Mastering the Catholic Liturgical Calendar

The Catholic ManBook contains the collective wisdom of The Men of the Immaculata, of saints, priests and laymen, fathers and sons, single and married. Holiness is at your fingertips. Get your copy today.

NEW! This year's edition also includes a revised and updated St. Louis de Montfort Marian consecration. Follow the prayers in a day-by-day format.

The Seventh Word

The FIRST Pro-Life Horror Novel!

Pro-Life hero, Abby Johnson, called it "legit scary ... I don't like reading this as night! ... It was good, it was so good ... it was terrifying, but good."

The First Word came with Cain, who killed the first child of man. The Third Word was Pharaoh's instruction to the midwives.

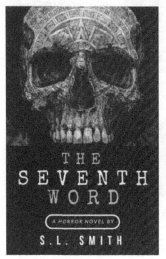

The Fifth Word was carried from Herod to Bethlehem. One of the Lost Words dwelt among the Aztecs and hungered after their children.

Evil hides behind starched white masks. The ancient Aztec demon now conducts his affairs in the sterile environment of corporate medical facilities. An insatiable hunger draws the demon to a sleepy Louisiana hamlet. There, it contracts the services of a young attorney, Jim David, whose unborn child is the ultimate object of the demon's designs. Monsignor, a mysterious priest of unknown age and origin, labors unseen to save the soul of a small town hidden deep within Louisiana's plantation country, nearly forgotten in a bend of the Mississippi River.

You'll be gripped from start to heart-stopping finish in this page-turning thriller.

With roots in Bram Stoker's Dracula, this horror novel reads like Stephen King's classic stories of towns being slowly devoured by an unseen evil and the people who unite against it.

The book is set in southern Louisiana, an area the author brings to life with compelling detail based on his local knowledge

Blessed is He Who ...
Models of Catholic Manhood

You are the average of the five people you spend the most time with, so spend more time with the Saints! Here are several men that you need to get to know whatever your age or station in life. These short biographies will give you an insight into how to live better, however you're living.

From Kings to computer nerds, old married couples to single teenagers, these men gave us extraordinary examples of holiness:

- Pier Giorgio Frassati & Carlo Acutis – Here are two extraordinary **young men**, an athlete and a computer nerd, living on either side of the 20th Century
- Two men of royal stock, Francesco II and Archduke Eugen, lived lives of holiness despite all the world conspiring against them.
- There's also the **simple husband and father**, Blessed Luigi. Though he wasn't a king, he can help all of us treat the women in our lives as queens.

Blessed Is He Who ... Models of Catholic Manhood explores the lives of six men who found their greatness in Christ and His Bride, the Church. In six succinct chapters, the authors, noted historian Brian J. Costello and theologian and attorney Scott L. Smith, share with you the uncommon lives of exceptional men who will one day be numbered among the Saints of Heaven, men who can bring all of us closer to sainthood.

THANKS FOR READING! TOTUS TUUS

Made in the USA
Monee, IL
05 October 2024

67238239R00104